Economics for Humans

ECONOMICS
for Humans

Julie A. Nelson

The University of Chicago Press
Chicago and London

JULIE A. NELSON is an economist at the Global Development and Environment Institute at Tufts University. She is author of *Feminism, Objectivity, and Economics*, coauthor of *Microeconomics in Context*, and coeditor of *Beyond Economic Man* and *Feminist Economics Today*.

The University of Chicago Press, Chicago 60637
The University of Chicago Press, Ltd., London
© 2006 by The University of Chicago
All rights reserved. Published 2006
Printed in the United States of America

15 14 13 12 11 10 09 08 07 06   1 2 3 4 5

ISBN-13: 978-0-226-57202-4 (cloth)
ISBN-10: 0-226-57202-1 (cloth)

Library of Congress Cataloging-in-Publication Data

Nelson, Julie A., 1956–
    Economics for humans / Julie A. Nelson.
        p. cm.
    Includes bibliographical references and index.
    ISBN 0-226-57202-1 (cloth : alk. paper)
    1. Economics—Moral and ethical aspects.   2. Economic man.
3. Feminist economics.   I. Title.

HB72.N445 2006
174—dc22

                                                          2005034406

♾ The paper used in this publication meets the minimum requirements of the American National Standard for Information Sciences—Permanence of Paper for Printed Library Materials, ANSI Z39.48-1992.

In memory of Martha E. Nelson (1923–2004)

Contents

Acknowledgments

If I personally thanked every person who has helped me on this book project, my acknowledgments would go on for far too many pages. Suffice it to say that my most grateful appreciation goes to my friends and fellow social scientists Nancy Folbre and Paula England. Iulie Aslaksen, Viviana Zelizer, and Nancy Tuana also provided inspiration and support at important junctures, while Sue Himmelweit and Lynn Stout were generous with comments. Dialogues with Ann-Cathrin Jarl, John B. Cobb Jr., Catherine Keller, and David Loy were invaluable in helping me refine my arguments concerning social ethics. The efforts of my editor at the University of Chicago Press, J. Alex Schwartz, brought this project to fruition.

Spending the 2000–2001 academic year as a fellow at the Center for the Study of Values in Public Life at Harvard Divinity School was crucial for getting this project rolling. Although the center no longer exists, I thank the selection committee, the many people from the larger Harvard community who commented on my work during that year, and my able research assistants, Rebecca Branch-Trevathan and Andrew Stern. The Foundation for Child Development and the Charlotte Perkins Gilman Fellowship for Research on Caring Labor also provided financial support, for which I am most grateful.

The book benefited greatly from the comments I received at various venues in North America and Europe, including at conferences of the International Association for Feminist Economics. I very much appreciate the supportive work environment I have enjoyed in recent years at the Global Development and Environment Institute at Tufts University.

Lastly, I would like to thank my Boston-area friends and "writing buddies" for their encouragement; my sister Laurie for letting me use her stories; and my children, Anne and Patrick, for their patience.

The views expressed in this book are my own and, of course, should not be assumed to represent the views of even these people and organizations to whom I owe a great debt.

Introduction

A very old definition of economics says that it is about the provisioning of goods and services to meet our material needs. That is, economics is about the way we manage our time and money so we can obtain groceries and shelter and thus "keep body and soul together."

In many discussions of economics, however, it seems that body and soul grow ever farther apart. A particular belief about commerce and its relation to ethics is implicit in many contemporary discussions, both academic and popular. This is the belief that money, profits, markets, and corporations are parts of an "economic machine." This machine operates in an automatic fashion, following inexorable and amoral "laws." While the machine organizes provisioning for our bodies, it is itself soulless and inhuman, according to this belief. Ethical questions, on the other hand, concern the appropriate respect and care for other creatures that we—as living, social, and soulful beings—should demonstrate. Since machines are incapable of morality, thinking about economies as machines puts commerce firmly outside the ethical realm. If this belief is true, then there is no point in worrying about the ethical implications of how we work and spend within contemporary capitalist or market-oriented economies.

Sometimes this belief takes a decidedly promarket form. "The capitalist economy can usefully be viewed as a machine whose primary product is economic growth," writes William Baumol, a distinguished economist, in a recent critically acclaimed book.[1] Free-market and probusiness advocates can be found in business, politics, and academia. Such advocates see market economies as nonhuman "engines" that nevertheless promote human well-being by meeting our bodily desires with an ever-increasing quantity and variety of material goods and services. They say that the eighteenth-century originator of economics, Adam Smith, showed that economies are driven by self-interest, and that he also showed that the "invisible hand" of the market will make such self-interest serve the common good. A direct consideration of ethics is rather irrelevant to economics, they infer, since good outcomes arise *automatically* from the operations of the "machine." As Doctor Pangloss asserted in Voltaire's *Candide*, we are "in the best of all possible worlds."

Sometimes this belief about the amoral economic machine comes with a decidedly antimarket or antibusiness slant. Because of the "logic" and "imperatives" of the world of money, David Korten, a popular critic of corporations writes, capitalism "has laid claim to our soul and is feeding on our flesh."[2] Contemporary economic life is systematically driven by greed and rampant materialism, such market critics say, and so is utterly opposed to the attainment of an ethical, meaningful social life.

People with a "critical," "alternative," or leftist view of society often believe that "business ethics" is an oxymoron—a contradiction in terms like "personal computer" (how personal can a computer be?) or "jumbo shrimp." They consider discussing ethical issues as they arise *within* the structure of capitalism to be largely a waste of time.

Sometimes holders of this belief in the economic machine are neither decidedly pro- or antibusiness in general, but instead divide the world into two parts. A state commissioner of social services has argued, for example, that his agencies shouldn't raise the rates they pay foster parents because "You don't want a cottage industry of professional foster parents for pay."[3] These people believe that certain realms of life must be kept in an ethically protected sphere, away from the motivations of self-interest. Activities especially rich in caring and human relationships such as child care, health care, and education are singled out for this special treatment. Other realms, they believe, can more or less safely be given over to the pecuniary interests that presumably drive normal economic life. These folks see a solution in the establishment of "separate spheres," with businesses left in charge of the commercial sphere and only nonprofits or government allowed within the protected sphere.

These views, in some ways, seem to be worlds apart. But they share a common base. Love it or leave it, these views join in claiming, there can be no ethical mucking-around with the fundamental "drives" of a monetized, corporatized, globalized, market-reliant economy.

I realize that not everyone will have the time (or perhaps inclination) to read this book in its entirety—so I'll cut to the chase. Here's the basic argument:

- The idea that economic systems are inanimate machines operating according to amoral laws is a *belief*, not a fact.
- This belief has harmful effects—for life on the planet, for human society, and for you in particular.
- Understanding that economies are vital, living, human-made, and shaped by our ethical choices can help to improve our decisions—both individually and as a society.

But perhaps your first question is simply: "Why should I listen to *you?*" After all, noted economists and other social scientists everywhere teach about "economic laws"—and sound thoughtful and rigorous doing so. You may firmly believe that contemporary economics correctly describes the "mechanisms" that "drive" market economic systems. The alternative of viewing economics as vital and laden with ethical meaning might sound to you . . . well, kind of squishy.

More likely, if you are reading this page, you already believe that *something* going on in contemporary economics is harmful for life on the planet and human society. You probably already see that current economic systems tend to be harsh, unsustainable, and unjust in many areas. You suspect that the promarket economics you learned in college or have picked up reading or listening to the news can't possibly be the whole story. Possibly, you have listened to some of the "alternative" economics voices but find it confusing when different people each identify a different "structure" or "mechanism" as being the one that is in dire need of fixing. Or you may be turned off when such discussions seem unrelentingly pessimistic or propose only utopian-sounding solutions.

You may work for a corporation and wonder if you should feel guilty. You may be an advocate for corporate social responsibility, but you are unsure how to defend your views. Conservatives don't think corporations need to aim for responsibility, so they put you down as a naive do-gooder. Meanwhile, radicals don't think corporations could ever be responsible, so they accuse you of selling out. Your "responsibility" position seems middle-of-the-road and wishy-washy, compared to those positions based on presumably rigorous "systemic" analysis. Or you may work in human services and wonder why your job requires you to make a personal financial sacrifice. You may be an advocate of better wages for people working in education, health care, or child care, but have a hard time countering the argument that such workers "shouldn't be in it for the money." You want well-thought-out and resilient arguments that you can use to articulate both your discomforts and your hopes, and you need ideas you can apply to practical life in the here-and-now.

So one reason you might want to listen to what I say in this book (at least on some matters) is that I must confess to being a professional economist. I have a Ph.D. in economics. I've worked as a government economist, and I've held a tenured faculty position in a respected economics department. As part of the drill, I've also published in professional journals, including the top ones in the discipline.[4] And I've taught economics at the undergraduate and graduate levels for over a decade. When the occasion demands, I can discuss esoteric topics with my colleagues. In other words, I've traveled to Oz—and seen behind the curtain.

As I ventured into economics, however, I brought two other important perspectives with me. One was a spiritual and ethical sensibility and concern with poverty and deprivation. Another is the fact that I'm a woman. Economics and commerce have traditionally been male-dominated realms, while women were traditionally assigned all the tasks of personal care for children and the ill and elderly within families.

If I were to try to live my life according to much of what I have been taught during my academic studies, I would have had to develop a personality split into three parts. My economist self would, like William Baumol, have had to admire the beauty of the economic machine. My ethical self would, like David Korten, have had to rail against the injustices generated by the economic juggernaut. My female self would, like the state commissioner, have needed to try to carve out a corner for personal concern and attention within the vast factory of impersonal economic life. The fact that I am determined *not* to live such a split life is what motivates me to write this book. For the sake of simplicity in writing, I will tend in this book to use the term *ethics* as shorthand for both concern with moral decision making and concern with interpersonal, caring relationships.

We are all deeply involved in corporate and business life, as consumers and often as workers or managers. We all have moral responsibilities. We all need care in our lives when we are young, sick, or elderly, and many of us also give care. I believe that, by carefully examining the history of the use of certain stale metaphors and images in the social sciences, we can come to see that economic gain and ethical values *aren't* by nature intrinsically separate or opposed.

First, I will present the issue from the side of those who prioritize economics and downplay ethics. Chapter 1, "Tending the Body," traces the history of economics from its early concern with bodily provisioning, through the mechanical imagery introduced by Adam Smith, and on to contemporary popular and academic economic discussions. One purpose of this chapter is to show that the metaphor of the mechanistic, amoral, clockwork economy has *particular* historical roots, and so to call into question the impression that it is a directly revealed truth. Another purpose is to show that values—both explicit and implicit—play important roles in a Panglossian probusiness worldview. Some of these values can be affirmed, while others, I will argue, should be considered with great suspicion.

Then I will turn the tables and look at the issue from the side of those who prioritize ethics and condemn (or seek to isolate) what they think of as "economic values." In chapter 2, "Tending the Soul," I trace the history of "critical" views in sociology and philosophy that developed in the early twentieth century. This history reveals that—far from reflecting a radically different perspective—the view of market critics is based on the *same* eighteenth-century Smithian metaphor as the probusiness view. As in the probusiness view, values both explicit and implicit play important roles in defining the approach of market critics. While some can be affirmed, I will show that others can legitimately be questioned.

Chapter 3, "Bringing Body and Soul Together," shows that the cause of the failure of the social sciences—and, as a result, much of public discourse—to adequately integrate economics and ethics lies in their failure to question the metaphorical image of the economy as a machine. I explain how historical and psychological factors have given the metaphor unusual—and mostly unconscious—power. I suggest that a vitalized metaphor that unites the provisioning and the ethical dimensions of economic life could be much more useful. Once the mechanical metaphor is set aside, there are legitimate values on which both "proeconomic" and "proethics" people can agree. In the present era of rapidly bifurcating red-state versus blue-state views, we need all the agreement we can get.

The next two chapters examine some of the many distorted or simply untrue beliefs about the facts of economic life that arise from the mechanical notion. Chapter 4, "Love *and* Money?" examines the issues of individual motivations and interpersonal relations. Can someone doing caring work also legitimately be in the job "for the money"? Can an employer hiring someone as a "human resource" also treat that person as a human? Some people say that the social sciences answer these questions in the negative. I dispute this view, arguing that "love *or* money" thinking is misleading and that generous evidence suggests that "love *and* money" is an important and realistic possibility.

In chapter 5, "Business *and* Ethics?" I take up the factual issues that arise at an organizational level. Don't legal mandates or market pressures *force* corporations to maximize profits? Shouldn't *non*profit organizations be the automatic choice for managing activities with caring and personal dimensions? Some people say that the social sciences answer these questions in the affirmative. I argue that ethical behavior is neither intrinsically at odds with organizational profit making nor guaranteed by nonprofit goals.

Lastly, chapter 6, "Keeping Body and Soul Together," draws conclusions for our actions as citizens, workers, parents, employers, and shareholders. Ironically and perversely, the misconception that caring work is different from—and needs to be protected from—the rest of economic life leads to the sectors of hands-on health care, early education, and social services being starved of vital economic resources. Perversely and ironically, the misconception that corporations *cannot* be ethical lets them off the hook for social responsibility, creating a permissive attitude for misbehavior. If we are to survive and flourish, as a species as well as individuals, we have to act as whole people, body and soul together.

I

TENDING THE BODY

The History of Economics

The Beginnings of Economics

The idea that part of life is "economic" has prosaic roots. The word *economic* comes from the Greek *oikos*, meaning "house," and *nomos*, meaning "to manage." An early use in English, the *Oxford English Dictionary* tells us, would be in a phrase such as "Doth employ her Oeconomick Art . . . her Household to preserve (1697)." The good household manager acts to preserve the household by making sure it stays provisioned with food and the other necessaries of life.

For much of human history, household economics for most of the population was largely a matter of self-provisioning, with the tasks ordered by slow-changing customs. The few in the ruling classes measured their wealth by land and gold. Economics came to be about provisioning and perhaps, secondarily, the taxation that provided the support for the ruling class. The merchant class was small.

The Industrial Revolution, beginning in England in the mid-eighteenth century, dramatically changed things. As it progressed, the organization of factory production and the development of markets for factory-produced goods brought a whole new dimension to provisioning relations. The broadened use of money and markets, the increasing importance of wage employment, and the new role played by financial and physical capital in sustaining industrial production transformed what had been a largely stagnant situation into one of massive, ongoing change. Wealth became increasingly identified with business production and profit. New classes formed: entrepreneurs and factory owners, on the one hand, and wage workers, on the other.

The "classical school" of economics arose from a desire to understand these emerging relations. The Scottish philosopher Adam Smith (1723–1790), by far the most prominent of the classical economists, was fascinated by the process of wealth creation. He wanted to explore how society was going about providing people with, as he wrote in 1776, the "necessaries and conveniences of life."[1] Smith's insights—about how the factory system used the division and specialization of labor and about the roles played by capital and markets—created the groundwork for understanding the new economic system of capitalism.

Yet the fact that classical economics rose during the time of the Industrial Revolution affected not only the *content* of what was studied (the capitalist industrial system) but also the *form* by which it was understood. The era of the rise of the factory was the era of the rise of the machine, predicated upon the somewhat earlier rise of science and technology.

This was a time of change in basic ways of perceiving the world. Up through the sixteenth century in Europe, the predominant conception of the relationship between humans and nature was primarily religious or, some might say, superstitious. People felt themselves to be embedded in a living cosmos. Religious rituals accompanied the sowing of seeds, the reaping of harvest, or the entry of a mineshaft into the living earth. Painting the picture in broad strokes, we can say that provisioning activities were shot through with understandings of the sacred. The fear of hell drove a preoccupation with the moral implications of every act. Scholarly study was primarily a matter of studying religious texts.

But then, starting with Galileo's (1564–1642) early work in mechanics, through René Descartes's (1596–1650) philosophical and mathematical elaborations, and finally Isaac Newton's (1643–1727) culminating work, the idea of the world as a sort of giant clockwork mechanism gained force. The physical aspects of the world were seen as reducible to components and forces describable in terms of laws and mathematics. Newton's Second Law of Motion summarized the relation of force, mass, and acceleration in a tidy calculus formula. The rise of science fomented the technological innovation that led to industrialization. It also radically changed the way people thought about the material world and how they thought about knowledge.

Not surprisingly, when Adam Smith described economic and political life in the eighteenth century, he used the popular mechanistic metaphors of his day. "Power and riches," he wrote, are "enormous and operose machines." The "wheels of the political machine," he continued, can be made to move in harmony when one attends to "the connexions and dependencies of its several parts."[2]

Smith is most noted, of course, for arguing that individuals' pursuit of their own self-interest is converted, by the mechanism of a self-regulating market system, into service to the good of others: "It is not from the benevolence of the butcher, the brewer, or the baker, that we expect our dinner," he wrote, "but from their regard to their own interest."[3] An individual acting from self-interest would be, he said, "led by an invisible hand" in the marketplace into the promotion of the social good.[4] While a fuller reading of Smith's work shows that he was actually a thinker who was much concerned with morals and saw roles for regulation of commerce, it is this idea of his that marks him as the originator of laissez-faire (free market) economics. Since Smith, self-interest has been assumed to be the "energy source" driving the "gears" of economic life.

As hard as it may be to believe from our contemporary standpoint, early scientists and economists generally did not see (or at least, given the power of the Church of their day, did not *acknowledge*) any conflict or even break of subject matter between science and the sorts of questions addressed by religion and philosophy. To most Enlightenment thinkers, the notion of nature as a clock was inseparable from the notion of God the Clockmaker. The world could be *both* mechanical *and* full of purpose and value, they thought, because it had purpose and value in God's eyes.

Later scientists and philosophers, however, increasingly noticed that, in fact, the study of the clockwork seemed to move along just fine without any notion of purpose, value, or ethics. The notion of a Clockmaker became increasingly irrelevant to scientific work. Darwinian evolutionary theory accelerated this process, by positing a mechanism other than once-and-for-all divine design by which the living parts of the clockwork might have been elaborated. Economists followed the same course, increasingly seeing their work as the objective study of the "drives" and "mechanisms" that run the economic "machine," rather than a study having anything to do with questions of a moral or spiritual nature.

Contemporary Probusiness Views

When you come across contemporary probusiness, promarket, and procapitalism arguments, you usually find that the highest priority is given to values such as those given in List I.

List I

- Production of goods and services that support survival and flourishing.
- Creation of employment opportunities.
- Self-support and financial self-responsibility.
- Opportunities for creativity, innovation, and growth in the enjoyment of life.

That is, such views emphasize the tremendous increases in material wealth that have come about in capitalist, market-oriented economies over the last two hundred or so years. Proponents of for-profit business see the opportunities and competitive discipline provided by relatively free-market economics as the driving forces behind this boom in prosperity. Business leaders are often—and often justly—proud of the goods they supply and the jobs their enterprises create. They often sincerely believe that the economy provides opportunities for every person to gain a good income and contribute to society—as long as he or she is willing to work. They put a high value on achieving autonomy and mastery. Superior rewards, probusiness advocates believe, go to those who not only labor but who also innovate and take risks.

Taken only this far, the *values* themselves are hard to completely dismiss, even if you disagree with the chain of thought
that ties them to a particular economic system. Whether your
ideal system is corporate capitalism or some other, perhaps
more socialistic or smaller-scale style of economy, doesn't there
seem to be something positive about valuing the items in List I?
Don't we need goods and services to live and be happy? Aren't
we distressed—often psychologically, by a feeling of useless-
ness, as well as financially—if we become unemployed? Don't
we feel that it's appropriate that people "pull their own weight,"
to the extent they are able? Don't many of us often yearn for a
creative outlet in our working life? I think the *values* promoted
by this view are ones we can all endorse to some extent, if we
think about them.

The more questionable part of the probusiness position
comes about when it is assumed that all good things are produced by the *automatic* functioning of the market system. That is,
taking a cue from Adam Smith, they assume that issues of ethics
need not be directly addressed because the "invisible hand" will
make even greed work for good. Some business leaders and
scholars of business are much more sophisticated in their thinking (I will discuss their work in chapter 3), but the promarket
zealotry that currently pervades much of popular discourse is
exactly of this simplistic sort. Probusiness advocates join with
Smith in their admiration of this magic of markets. As Smith
wrote, "The perfection of [policy], the extension of trade and
manufactures, are noble and magnificent objects. . . . We take
pleasure in beholding the perfection of so beautiful and grand a
system, and we are uneasy till we remove any obstruction that
can in the least disturb or encumber the regularity of its

motions."[5] The "obstructions" that many contemporary free-market advocates seek to remove include governmental regulations, business taxes, and restrictions on international trade that, they believe, create a drag on the creation of wealth. They also oppose redistributive taxation and social welfare payments that, they believe, make less perfect the mechanism that leads from individual effort to individual reward. Even deliberate actions on the part of corporations to be socially responsible may be seen as gumming up the works, since they take energy away from the drive for profits that leads to the best of all possible worlds. Poverty, unemployment, social distress, and environmental damage, they believe, arise not from the workings of the system, but from obstructions put in its way. Take away government "interference" and other encumbrances, they say, and the free-market system will create wealth for all.

Before I turn to the subject of how this popular worldview has been buttressed by work in academic economics, let me take a moment to explain how these probusiness folks are likely to perceive their critics. They tend to perceive anyone who questions their arguments as an unrealistic idealist who doesn't recognize the value of what the economy has created—the value of those things laid out in List I. They assume that you don't adequately appreciate how the economy has lifted many people from poverty, or that you are a nonindustrious person—a granola-eating hippie-type, perhaps—not willing to shoulder your load. They may—perhaps with some reason—think that you are naive because your base is in the ivory tower of academe or the hallowed halls of religious or nonprofit institutions. There you rest on money raised by taxes or donations, walled off from the hurly-burly of the practical business world.

If you don't agree with them about the priority that should be given to the items in List I, they assume, in short, that you must display characteristics like those on List II.

List II
- Passivity about provisioning of goods and services.
- Otherworldliness, with little attention to practical needs or constraints.
- Financial nonresponsibility, leading to dependency.
- Fear of money and power.

Some business groups express anger toward academic institutions and departments that they consider to be hotbeds of left-leaning, egg-headed, out-of-touch, antibusiness (and thus "anti-American," in this country) intellectuals. These List II characteristics generally play a role in their list of complaints. Business leaders see the conflict as one of values—of activity and provisioning that lead to betterment of human life, versus characteristics of laziness and idealistic otherworldliness that undervalue and undermine all that they have accomplished.

Needless to say, the low opinion probusiness people hold of their opponents does not create a good foundation for dialogue. But my own life experiences have urged me to look for more adequate ways of thinking about economic life.

Entering the World of Economics

I didn't know, growing up, that I wanted to be an economist. My dream as a little girl, in the early 1960s, was more along the stereotypical ballerina line. I stumbled into taking economics at college—although, for a while, I was not sure I would be going to college at all.

My mother had come down with rheumatoid arthritis when she was in her twenties, and, by the time I was in grade school, she relied on crutches to get around. My two older sisters, each in turn, took on the routines of helping my mother dress, doing the shopping, cooking dinner for the family, and running errands. Once my sisters were both away at college, the routines fell to me. But since I was the youngest, if I went away to college, who would take over? As it turned out, my education was not a subject on which my parents were prepared to make compromises. A female cousin was recruited as my replacement. I was off the hook and off to St. Olaf, a Lutheran college in Minnesota.

As was typical in those precomputerized days, we freshmen were herded en masse onto the floor of the new athletic center to register for classes. Folding tables had been set up, each with a cardboard sign raised on a dowel advertising the name of a department. Chalkboards behind each table listed the classes that had already filled. I had put down "undecided" on the forms where I was supposed to list a major and had been, rather arbitrarily, assigned a historian as an advisor. I sat across from him on a cold metal chair with the blank registration form in front of me. We easily filled in classes to meet requirements in math, religion, and language.

"What about your social science requirement?" my advisor asked. "Any idea what area interests you?"

"I'm kind of interested in psychology," I replied.

No luck. The introductory psychology classes were all filled up and closed.

"I think you'd enjoy trying economics," my adviser said and more or less frog-marched me over to the Economics table. All the introductory classes that would fit my schedule were filled, I saw with a tinge of relief. I associated economics with business, and business with greed, and—as a Lutheran minister's daughter—this didn't exactly fit my values or my self-image. But my advisor was a friend of the faculty member who taught an intro economics class that, though full, did fit my schedule. After some chatting between them, I found myself signed into the course on an override.

Like many of the other students at that church-associated school, I entered it aspiring to a life of service of one kind or another. St. Olaf produces many doctors, nurses, and ministers. My father had wanted me to go into pre-med and become a medical missionary. I was unsure about the medical aspect of this plan but felt drawn to it in principle. My economics professors at St. Olaf were largely warm, humane, and intelligent people who believed that teaching this subject was consistent with such values. After I found out that economics was a social science— a way of understanding in broad terms how human social behavior might be organized—I came to drop my association of it with business management. I thought that perhaps it would help me contribute to solving problems of global poverty. Now I developed a vague idea that, perhaps, instead of going into medicine I could help figure out why there were so few good hospitals in poor countries and how economic systems could be changed to increase people's health. I also liked the fact that the study of economics allowed me to use my skills in mathematics.

And so I began my studies in academic economics.

The Development of Academic Economics

Academic economists have taken the mechanical metaphor for economics very, *very* seriously. John Stuart Mill (1806–1873) asserted that economists must base their knowledge of the production of wealth on "laws of human nature," equivalent to the "laws of motion" found by scientists who study physical mechanics. In order to practice economics as a science, Mill argued, it would be useful for economists to assume "an arbitrary definition of man, as a being who inevitably does that by which he may obtain the greatest amount of necessaries, conveniences, and luxuries, with the smallest quantity of labour and physical self-denial with which they can be obtained" or "who desires to possess wealth, and who is capable of judging the comparative efficacy of means for obtaining that end."[6] This concept later came to be summarized by the term "economic man." "Economic man" is an individual rational calculator interested only in his own material or financial gain.

In the late nineteenth century, some scholars began formulating Smith's and Mill's ideas in mathematical terms. The first "neoclassical" economists included Francis Edgeworth (1845–1926), William Stanley Jevons (1835–1882), Leon Walras (1834–1910), and Vilfredo Pareto (1848–1923). They explicitly borrowed their calculus-based models directly from earlier developments in mechanical physics. The idea gained ground that business firms are entities that produce goods, acting like "economic man" in making calculations that maximize their mathematical profit function. Expenses and revenues are both measured in monetary terms, so the application of math to the topic of profits seemed to follow directly.

Households posed a slightly more difficult problem. They receive a mathematically measurable monetary income, it is true. But the neoclassical economists' problem was to explain how households make consumption decisions. It is not obvious that all of a household's purchases of oranges, bicycles, and haircuts "add up" to something that can be measured in a common unit. So here the neoclassical economists had to get a little more creative. They invented "utility" as something that a household could maximize. They assumed that all household decisions were for the purpose of raising a single number representing "utility" (or satisfaction) to its highest possible value. Having created this fiction, neoclassical economists assumed that households solved mathematical problems analogous to those solved by profit-maximizing firms.

Firms and households were envisioned as interacting on free, competitive markets, where only offers to buy and sell need be communicated. Offers would take the form of paired numerical values of monetary price and physical quantity. Prices and quantities at which deals take place would be automatically determined by market forces, settling at the levels dictated by conditions of supply and demand. The concepts of economics were assumed to be direct counterparts to the concepts of physical science—profit, utility, and prices were compared to particles, raised and lowered by the impersonal forces of market interaction.

Forcing analysis of human behavior into these mathematical molds meshed elegantly with Smith's earlier image of the clockwork economy. The notion of economies as impersonal, machinery-like entities directly amenable to "scientific" study was clinched when human beings were recast as robots whose conduct could be described by simple mathematical formulas. In the 1930s, economist Lionel Robbins offered his precedent-setting definition of economics as the science of *choice-making* in the face of unlimited wants and scarce resources. Within academic economics, the classical emphasis on wealth and its creation and distribution increasingly gave way to a neoclassical emphasis on the calculus of rational choice.

As the coup de grace, even Smith's claim that automatic market operations *serve the social good* came to be mathematically "proven" by the neoclassical economists. The economics subdiscipline of "welfare economics" does not deal with government programs, as one might expect, but rather with abstract theories about what sorts of economic arrangements serve to maximize social well-being. The so-called First Fundamental Theorem of Welfare Economics is usually taken to state, in layperson's terms, that free-market economies give us the best of all possible worlds. The theorem "shows" that interference in free markets leads only to social harm.[7] Thus, neoclassical theory gives formal, academic support to the free-marketeering views espoused in public and media discussions.

Nowadays, the core curriculum for economics at most American and European (and many other) universities is based on this neoclassical model. Undergraduates study neoclassical theory, usually not realizing that what they see presented as economic knowledge is not based on economists' years of intensive study of actual businesses and households. Rather, the base is actually a set of mathematically convenient assumptions and Smith's image of a mechanically driven economy. Beginning economics students learn rules such as "set marginal revenue equal to marginal cost." At more advanced and graduate levels, the underlying model becomes a little clearer. Once students have had calculus, the faculty introduce the actual mathematical functions from which the rules that students memorized earlier were derived. It's all very elegant, in a geekish sort of way.[8]

The mechanical image is so deeply ingrained in academic economics that its status as a *particular* image, that is, a *particular* way of looking at things, is rarely presented as open to question. Neoclassical theory is usually presented not as one theory to be considered in relation to others, but as the direct "truth" about the way a market economy functions at its core. To raise a challenge would be, after all, to question the "laws of human nature"! The separation of economics from ethics now seems entirely natural to many people. To my mainstream economist colleagues, economics is a positive science that seeks to understand the mechanisms underlying economic systems. Ethics, to them, seems like a soft, subjective topic, necessarily encompassing value judgments and ambiguity. Ethics is not, in their perception, a "hard" field, like their own, which starts with objective, "value-free" premises and then logically derives clear, precise, and defensible results. Most economists believe that economic science can proceed just fine without attention to ethics.

Values in Academic Economics

As I mentioned earlier, businesspeople often defend capitalism because they highly value provisioning, employment creation, self-reliance, and innovation. What is the value base of academic economists' mechanical modeling?

Most neoclassical economists would be loath to admit that their analysis is value-based at all. They vary in the degree to which they believe their core model can be used to directly guide public policy, and many in fact disagree with the policies proposed by the free-market populists. Instead of political loyalty, it has largely been a drive to achieve mathematical elegance and physics-mimicking "scientificity" that has guided the elaboration of the machine metaphor within the academic world.

I have already given one explicit example of this in the case of Mill. He was a broad philosopher who certainly knew better than to think that people were as narrow as "economic man" in general. But he argued for the use of that assumption in economics because he believed that economics as a *science* would best progress from the use of clear assumptions and deductions. We can further see how much this priority given to the purity of deductive and mathematical methods has driven economics by looking at some of the "fine print" on the First Fundamental Theorem of Welfare Economics mentioned earlier.

Most people would probably assume that the criteria for social welfare should include such things as meeting people's basic survival needs and not destroying the life-supporting ecological processes of the planet. Not so in the world of neoclassical economics. Because of the desire to keep economics as "objective" and "value-free" as possible, economists have adopted a rather bizarre notion of social well-being or welfare. They have gone out of their way to avoid any criteria that could possibly be thought of as "subjective," fearing that their "science" would be tainted if they made "value judgments."

"Needs," this school has claimed, for example, cannot be *scientifically* distinguished from "wants." Who is to say, for example, that dental care is a "need," if so many people around the world get along without it? With no *clear, scientific* way to draw the line between needs and wants, neoclassical economics has dispensed with the concept of "need" entirely. Concerns about the environment, the healthiness of consumption patterns, or the justness of the distribution of income have all likewise been set aside, because these are concerns about which people sometimes disagree. Also set aside have been questions about the well-being effects of corporate power, media advertising, histories of colonialism, problems of misinformation and dishonesty, and many other factors a thoughtful person might consider to be important in judging the performance of an economic system.

The criterion of welfare or well-being in the neoclassical model has been pared down to the single, narrow issue of efficiency in the use of resources. Presumably, everyone would agree that getting the most value from a given set of resources (that is, being efficient) is better than getting less value. Therefore, economists have reasoned, minimizing waste is the one universal value that can be defended on "objective" and "scientific" grounds. The so-called welfare theorem simply says that *perfectly* functioning "free markets" lead to an *efficient* outcome. It says nothing about what happens if markets are complex and messy and nothing about issues of fairness, health, survival, or sustainability.

The model is simply set up such that everything that is not "scientifically" justified and mathematically tractable is assumed away. By attempting to create a certain kind of "value-free" or "objective" approach amenable to mathematical treatment, neoclassical economics in fact, by omission, *de*valued concern with human needs, justice, and sustainability.

Neglecting the Body

Thus, oddly enough, as academic economics turned toward an emphasis on "economic man" and his calculations, the original emphasis on provisioning for real human bodies increasingly fell away. I had hoped, in entering economics, to find some knowledge relevant to the problem of poverty. What I found, instead, in my years of graduate classes, were endless mathematical elaborations of a machine-based metaphor.

So how are human bodies actually doing in contemporary capitalist societies? Examining the evidence, you can find much that calls into question the idea that market functioning automatically brings about social well-being. Of course, the richer you are and the more you have benefited from the system, the more you may be likely to see the market system through rose-colored glasses. But at the other extreme, the World Health Organization says that fifteen thousand children per day die worldwide from malnutrition-related diseases.You only have to read the business news to find reports on corporate abuses worldwide, including inhumane labor standards, egregious pollution, and the use of violence to suppress dissent. Organizations such as CorpWatch and Corporation Watch provide additional detail. Corruption at Enron, WorldCom, and the like wiped out the retirement savings of employees and outside investors and has shaken people's faith in the honesty of corporate leaders. A 2001 congressional report found that almost one in three U.S. nursing homes—many of them making good profits—had been cited for abuse violations. The Intergovernmental Panel on Climate Change and many other scientists warn us that global warming is real and is caused largely by our fossil-fuel-based economic growth.

Perhaps the most dramatic episode in recent history concerns what happened in Russia after the fall of Communism. Many economists expected that free markets would simply blossom once the "encumbrances" of state control were lifted from Russian society. They thought that the "natural forces" and "economic laws" of capitalism, now unleashed, would more or less *automatically* create the grand system first described by Adam Smith. What developed instead, as we know, was chaos, corruption, fraud, murder, and an economy that has had more in common with organized crime than with organized markets. Rates of poverty and alcoholism climbed, while Russian male life expectancy dropped to 58 years.

Even some economists are now starting to consider the idea that a well-functioning market system might be something more than a machine driven by self-interest. Some are beginning to think that perhaps an economy needs to pay attention to ethical norms and social ties and create well-designed human institutions, if it is to generate wealth.[9]

I've raised many issues in this chapter that I will be coming back to—and sometimes arguing with or refuting—later on. But for now, let's keep our eye on the mechanical image of economic functioning and look at how it spread through the other social sciences and popular thought.

2

TENDING THE SOUL

The Defense of "Noneconomic Values"

A Surprising Agreement

It didn't hit me until I was well into being an economics major how sorely the discipline neglects important aspects of how we support ourselves and sustain our lives. Mainstream economics really had nothing to say of any intelligence about the economic relations characterizing the life I had led at home, caring for my mother. I quickly learned that the "appropriate" questions to ask in economics classes were about math and graphs. Human connections, human needs, and the appropriate ethical responses to these were left to other fields.

So, when I got a chance, I started to investigate other fields. "Surely fields like sociology, psychology, theology, literature, and philosophy must deal more appropriately with human interdependencies," I thought. "Surely *they* can't be formed around the images of 'economic man' and mechanical markets."

In some ways I was correct. Looking into the field of the psychology of human development, for example, I found the following description of what happens during early education:

> Child development research indicates that preschool teachers who are warm, responsive, and engage in one-to-one relationships have positive effects on children's learning. For the preschool child, the "subjects" are all combined and integrated into a whole and learned simultaneously. Brain development research suggests that the strongest element for successful teaching at any level is the ability to form relationships and the ability to be responsive.[1]

So here, and in other places, I have found discussions of relationships, responsiveness, care, and warmth. I have found discussions of ethics, meaning, and concern for those in need. Reading further, I've found awareness of our deep human links to our natural world and a sensitivity to ecological balance. And these aren't just instances of Hallmark card sentimentality. The passage about child development, for example, is based on actual neuroscience research. In these other fields, real human emotions, connections, and dependencies can sometimes be a valid topic of scholarly study.

What has surprised me, however, is that I have often found that the people who are so articulate about care and relationships in their own field apparently *fully agree* with Adam Smith, John Stuart Mill, and neoclassical economists when the topic turns to economics. They believe that people can and should be caring and moral in some contexts. When the topic is the economic aspects of life, however, they go along with the idea that people are helpless in the face of "economic laws" and inevitably become self-interested calculators. They agree that markets and for-profit firms function in a sphere where values such as responsibility and compassion, values that we demand in other parts of our life, do not apply. They do not question the idea that markets are machines driven by self-interest.

For example, I've had opportunities to engage with a number of religious ethicists. One of the leading European Christian ethicists, John Atherton, an Anglican priest, argues that ethicists need to defer to economists' knowledge of the "mechanisms and systems" that make up "the reality of the relatively autonomous world of economics."[2] The implication is that economy must be left to run along its "lawful" lines. The most ethicists and concerned religious people can do, apparently, is seek to remedy some of the economic machine's most egregious damages and injustices after the fact. Ethics, in this interpretation, is a mop-up operation.

The same idea also appears in discussions with a more overtly critical slant. Writer David Korten's popular book *When Corporations Rule the World* has encouraged thousands of readers to think of corporations as nonhuman "aliens" or "machines" that are part of a "badly corrupted global economic system that is gyrating far beyond human control." Feminist political theorist Nancy Fraser writes about "relatively autonomous markets" that "follow a logic of their own" separated from culture and values. Buddhist scholars have followed suit: David Loy describes economies in terms of "engines" fired up by greed, while Ken Jones describes capitalism as a structure or system driven by "the logic of the market" and writes that it must be "dismantled." Celebrated novelist and ecological essayist Barbara Kingsolver draws on the ingrained metaphor when she describes commerce as "simply an engine with no objective but to feed itself." Philosopher Virginia Held is one of a large group of humanists and social scientists who worry that goods and services with unique human value (such as child care) inevitably become "commodified" if they are provided by businesses—because the profit motive, of course, drives business life. Historian and advocate of community-based development Gar Alperovitz writes that the inherent "logic and dynamics of the capitalist system" are to blame for ecologically unsustainable outcomes.[3] I could go on and on.

Contemporary Market-Critic Views

These critics of markets, corporations, or capitalism accept the notion that market systems are mechanisms bound to the logic of competitive market forces and fueled by the energy of self-interest. What they want to do is *defend* what they see as important dimensions of human life against what they call "economic" or "market" values.

If you come upon such arguments, you will usually find that values like those in List III are given highest priority:

List III
- Aesthetic, moral, and spiritual development.
- The creation of emotionally healthy, mutually respectful relations among people.
- Care and concern for the weak and needy.
- Ecological balance and sustainability.

That is, such market critics are concerned with all that gives *meaning* to life. They are concerned about interpersonal relations, emotions, and real communication. They are concerned not only about the independent "agent" or "citizen," but about the weak and needy, the elderly, the sick, and the very young. The description of the demands of preschool teaching, for example, draws directly on the first three items in the list. Often, the attention to interrelations extends to questions of our interrelations with the natural world, bringing in ecological concerns.

These *values* are hard to dismiss. In fact, they are great. Only the most hard-core, shallow, selfish fiend, it would seem, would say that these values are unimportant in creating a life worth living. Ebenezer Scrooge in *A Christmas Carol* provides an old cautionary tale about the first three values. From being a fringe idea in the 1960s, the valuing of ecological balance has now become more mainstream, with issues like global warming attracting increasing public attention.

What is more questionable about the market critics' views is that these values are often set up *in opposition to* a model of mechanical commercial life. What they see as "economic values" tend to be something like List IV.

List IV
- An exclusive focus on short-term profit.
- Creation of boss/worker relations of oppression and alienation.
- Greed and selfishness.
- A fixation on growth and runaway consumerism.

The oppositional pairing of lists III and IV leads to the implication that if you are interested in profit, you simply cannot also be interested in moral values. If you are a boss, the possibility of emotionally healthy, respectful relationships with your employees is made impossible by the intrinsic dynamics of capitalism. If you are interested in money, you must be greedy and selfish and not concerned about the weak and needy. People who prioritize List III tend to think of themselves as promoting "higher values" of spirituality, morality, and meaning. They tend to disdain the viewpoints of those concerned with the "lower values" of materialism and money. They tend to look on people who think positively about business, money, and profit as selfish—or perhaps, at best, as merely sadly deluded.

This doesn't create much foundation for dialogue between the antimarket and probusiness factions. In fact, the prescriptions for change that come from these antimarket folks focus on *beating back* the economic machine. Their three main solutions can be characterized as Small Is Beautiful, Government to the Rescue, and Separate Spheres (though many market critics subscribe to some combination).

Small Is Beautiful. One highly popular variant of dualistic thinking sees our current economic system as intrinsically either immoral (evil) or amoral (set apart from questions of morality). "Small is beautiful" advocates want to replace our current system with a system or structure thought to be, in contrast, intrinsically moral. Our current system is characterized by competition, this story goes, so a new system must run by cooperation. Our current economic structure gives a lot of power to large corporations, so we need to convert to small-scale, community-based economies. Our current economy is driven by profit, so we need to replace it with an economy run according to human needs. These advocates want a wholesale "systemic" or "structural" change toward nonprofit community enterprises. David Korten's ideal of "localizing economies" and Herman Daly and John Cobb's economy "for the common good" are perhaps the best-known contemporary examples.[4]

Government to the Rescue. The "small is beautiful" argument, however, requires such radical change that I have noticed that it is often paired with another seemingly more practical argument which I will call "government to the rescue." Many critics allow that, alongside truly alternative structures, it might be all right to allow for-profit businesses and even large global corporations to continue to function—as long as they're tightly kept in line by public-interested governments. Writer Marjorie Kelly, for example, argues that governments should rewrite corporate charters so that they require employee participation in decision making and accountability to the public good.[5] Myriad new possible government regulations have been proposed to *force* companies into better social or environmental behaviors. Or it may be proposed that governments simply take over many important economic activities that are currently managed privately, in order to directly run them for the public good.

Separate Spheres. Another variant of the markets-are-immoral-mechanism view sees them slightly more favorably. Part of the economy, these "separate spheres" advocates suggest, can more or less safely be given over to "market values." Presumably amoral, mechanical markets can be allowed to operate in some realms where efficiency is highly valued—say, in the provision of consumer goods. But some realms of economic provisioning should be walled off from contamination from profit-oriented values and held to higher standards. As mentioned earlier, health care, education, and child care are among those spheres that are often thought of as needing protection from "commodification." Hence, a sort of separate-sphere economy is proposed, with some sectors left to relatively free-wheeling capitalism, while in the protected spheres only public (à la "government to the rescue") or nonprofit or community (à la "small is beautiful") organizations are allowed to operate.[6]

These prescriptions all agree that the capitalist economy is a machine. They merely differ about whether the machine should be dismantled, controlled by the state, or enclosed within containment walls.

The Origins of the Iron Cage

While the popular probusiness view is buttressed by the theories of academic neoclassical economics, the market-critic view gets its intellectual support from academic sociology and philosophy. Eminent sociologist Max Weber (1864–1920) wholeheartedly adopted the mechanical metaphor for economic life, and created a now-famous variation on this image. The economic order, he wrote, "is now bound to the technical and economic conditions of machine production which to-day determine the lives of all the individuals who are born into this mechanism. . . . [While, in the view of another writer] the care for external goods should only lie on the shoulders of the 'saint like a light cloak' . . . fate decreed that the cloak should become an iron cage."[7] The idea that life under industrial capitalism has become an "iron cage" has carried tremendous weight.

Critical theorist Jürgen Habermas (1929–), drawing on earlier work by Karl Marx (1818–1883), Weber, and others, took up the charge in the late twentieth century. He has made an influential distinction between what he has called the "lifeworld" and the "system." The lifeworld, he has written, is the sphere of morals, aesthetics, and conscious action. In families, neighborhoods, and democratic public participation, he has claimed, people exercise freedom and responsibility, in a context rich with meaning and formative of identity and personality. Capitalist economies, on the other hand, are part of the "system," driven by unconscious, objectifying forces, as suggested by Weber's "iron cage" metaphor and Marx's idea of the intrinsic dynamics of capital accumulation. The market economy is not organized by people, according to Habermas's theory, but rather is "steered" by the "media" of money. Like Marx, Habermas believes that relations among people working together in a capitalist business are inherently alienating. He believes that such relations become stripped of their human dimensions and are ordered only by the media of money and power.[8]

The economy functions independently of human norms and personality, as an autonomous sphere with its own "internal systemic logic" and "drive mechanism," in Habermas's view. However, he believes that the system is not all bad. The system is, in fact, a complex and effective way of providing material goods. What Habermas thinks *is* dangerous, is that the ways of thinking and media appropriate to the economic system inevitably, by their own "irresistible inner dynamics," infiltrate the lifeworld. This "colonization" of the lifeworld, as he has called it, destroys freedom, meaning, and ethics, making life "technicized" and "norm-free." Hence, he has written, any incursion of profit interests or money into areas of the lifeworld should be resisted.

Advocates of a "separate spheres" prescription can thus find intellectual ammunition for their position in the work of this influential thinker. Because Habermas borrowed some concepts from Marx, this position is often considered to be "leftist" or "critical." Certainly, in one way this perspective and Adam Smith's seem to be miles apart. While Adam Smith emphasized the harmony and wealth he believed came from the economic system, Habermas's view emphasizes how economic life threatens us with depersonalization. In fact, however, as Habermas explicitly states in his work, his mechanical image of the economy is *directly derived* from Adam Smith. He credits Smith as being the originator of system theory.[9] As far as intellectual history goes, the root of this market-critic view is *exactly the same as* the root of the probusiness view described in the last chapter.

The idea that the world of morals and care is distinct from the world of business has also had an interesting *gender* dimension in both popular life and scholarly thought. During the Victorian era, middle-class women were thought to be the guardians of morals and care, which were assumed to rule in the home. Meanwhile, men were thought to be morally less pure by nature and hence appropriately assigned to the rough-and-tumble world of competitive business. Sociologist Arlie Hochschild has summarized this ideology in a recent book, stating, "When in the mid-nineteenth century, men were drawn into market life and women remained outside it, female homemakers formed a moral brake on capitalism."[10] Hochschild does not present this social division as an ideology, however, but rather presents it as though it were fact. Portraying the world as divided into a harsh, depersonalized, masculine world of intrinsically destabilizing materialism and capitalism on the one hand, and an ethical, caring-laden sphere of authentic, nonmonetized family and community relations on the other is a popular theme. Sometimes such thinkers believe that it is now "up to women" to hold the line against capitalist incursion or to lead a movement into a softer, more feminized, small-is-beautiful, and soulful economic system.

Whether they explicitly cite Weber, Marx, and Habermas, or draw on Victorian ideology, some variety of this idea that capitalism is intrinsically incompatible with relational and ethical values is at the heart of the arguments of the market critics.

Problems with the Market-Critic Prescriptions

At the end of the last chapter, I brought up evidence of poverty and corporate abuses that raise questions about the adequacy of the probusiness, free-market prescription for curing social ills. Do the prescriptions of the market critics for "small is beautiful," "government to the rescue," or "separate spheres" solutions give us grounds for more hope?

The "small is beautiful" prescription contains, of course, some truth. It is true that acting ethically is a more *complicated* process the larger and more complex the level of organization involved. Likewise, the "government to the rescue" advocates make some good points. It is easier for any one company to do the right thing if there is public pressure on all companies to do the right thing, and a government regulation can be a good tool for applying such pressure. On an even larger scale, international public agreements may be the only hope for addressing global climate change issues. These are far too big for any one nation, let alone one company, to take on. And there is some truth in the "separate spheres" view. There are some social welfare problems for which private, market solutions don't work. Care for people who are poor and ill or otherwise needy cannot be provided on a purely market basis. The funds have to come from somewhere other than the "consumers" of the services. Public or private nonprofit allocations of money are necessary.

But while the values held in high regard by market critics are praiseworthy, and the prescriptions contain partial truths, I find the prescribed solutions lacking when held up to criteria of realism and effectiveness. Sometimes the proposed solutions could cause real damage.

A first problem is that these views tend to assume not only that the market sphere is driven *exclusively by* self-interest, but that self-interest is *exclusive to* the market sphere. They often seem to assume that if an organization is small, or nonprofit, or governmental, then non-self-interested motivations can be trusted to take over. We should consider the evidence on this.

Families, for example, are very small nonprofit organizations, presumably governed by interests of love and intimacy (as in the Victorian image). The newspaper reminds us daily, however, that families can also be characterized by domination and abuse, even violence. Sometimes being in a small-scale organization just means being under the thumb of a small-scale oppressor.

Community organizing is a great way to bring a group together to work on issues of social concern and to create opportunities for activism. Community organizing was very effective in South Boston in the 1970s, for instance, when big community demonstrations were organized to *fight* racial integration of the local public schools. Sometimes community groups carry out agendas of racism. And it is not uncommon for community activists motivated by not-in-my-backyard sentiments to try to push undesirable projects off on some other community. Communities, like individuals, can act in purely self-interested ways.

Nonprofit and religious organizations can bring people together to work for goals other than profit. The Boston diocese of the Catholic Church, for example, is legally not allowed to be motivated by profit. It was the maintenance of its own institutional hierarchies and reputation that motivated it to quietly move priests who sexually abused children from one parish to another, thereby supplying the abusers with fresh victims. Non-profit institutions—even those ostensibly concerned with maintaining moral and spiritual values—are not immune to evil.

In an era of suspicious elections, campaign finance fiascos, and powerful lobbyists, one has to be naive in the extreme to believe that governments can be trusted to automatically or naturally work for the common good.

Appeals to small communities, nonprofits, or governments to take over economic activities "in the public interest" seem to me to bring in a *deus ex machina* solution. Yes, it would be nice if it worked. But how do we know that those selfish motivations critics assume drive the market are not *also* going to show up in families, community organizations, nonprofits, and the state?

A second problem with these views is that they largely pull the rug out from under their own noble drives. Because money and power are associated with greed and oppression, money and power are treated as inherently morally suspect. People who possess these, such as corporate executives who might be willing to engage in ethical discussion (if given the chance), are labeled as the evil "them," separated by a large gulf from the moral "us." Thus, potential allies and power bases are eliminated. This aversion to money and power has, I believe, been especially damaging to the sectors of the economy in which hands-on care is provided to children, the sick, and the elderly. Remember this poster: "It will be a great day when the schools have all the money they need and the air force has to hold a bake sale to buy a bomber"? How true. But the antimoney ideology reinforces exactly the bake-sale, nickel-and-dime mentality for human services that that poster decried. The damage this attitude has inflicted on caring work will be taken up further when I look at issues of money and motivations in chapter 4.

A third problem is that, even if the prescriptions given by market critics were viable once put in place, there would still remain the problem of getting there. The massive promarket tide now flooding the United States and global institutions presents an intimidating reality check. The "small is beautiful" view tells us that we must have a massive economic restructuring—the thorough destruction of large corporations as a form of economic organization—before we can really be human in our economic lives. This would require a gargantuan change—larger, perhaps, than the Industrial Revolution and the rise and fall of Communism combined. If, on the other hand, we hope to be rescued by the rise of powerful, purely public-spirited interventionist governments, the current political climate makes it look like we may be waiting a very long time. Every step toward wresting control away from those with money and power will, market critics correctly perceive, be resisted by those with money and power.

Some people enjoy tilting at the economic machine—or at windmills, like Don Quixote in his hopeless crusades. In fact, I admire the spirit of people who keep to their praiseworthy, treasured values against all odds. But what if the futures envisioned by market critics, visions that tend to seesaw between the utopian and apocalyptic, are not the only options? What if the proposed solutions are unsatisfactory because the market critics have, unfortunately, combined good values with erroneous "facts" about what an economy *is*?

3

BRINGING BODY

AND SOUL TOGETHER

Being an Unusual Economist

Here is where a chance for real fresh and useful thinking about ethics and economics opens up: Do we *have* to believe that the economy is a machine? Do we have to believe that self-interest is its sole "natural" energy source? The image is so familiar to us and so tied up for centuries with our notions of science-as-mechanics that it may be hard to think about what economic knowledge would look like if that image were dropped. Letting go of this "hard" image of what economies are might seem threatening. Especially to those who study economies, moving away from the "rigor" and "precision" provided by mathematical tools based on Newtonian physics might seem to lead us, as mentioned earlier, into a morass of soft-headed thinking.

But I had an advantage when I began my study of economics: I was the "wrong" gender. The field of economics has historically been dominated by men. At the time I entered graduate school in 1980, only 12 percent of Ph.D. degrees in economics were awarded to women. I dove into the pool of graduate study in economics as one of only four women in an entering class of thirty-five. I found it to be a peculiar environment. My male colleagues didn't find it so peculiar, but then, I've heard it said that fish don't know they are living in water.

While working hard to keep up with the endless mathematical problem sets required in my courses, I also kept mental notes on a more subtle object of learning. This was the internal value system of the profession. What was I being taught to respect, and what was I being taught to disregard? As noted in chapter 1, mathematical sophistication is held in undisputed high regard. And this value led to other things being treated with disdain. We hardly ever read anything written with just *words*, for example. A lack of Greek letters and mathematical symbols was taken to be a sign of weakness. Economic agents were assumed to be autonomous, rational, and self-interested. Issues of human need or dependency, emotion, or care did not enter into discussions at all, being considered nonrigorous and sentimental. It became increasingly clear to me that, far from being an unbiased study of how we provide for ourselves, academic economics was in fact built around a whole structure of biased beliefs. The undercurrent I detected can be broadly summarized as follows:

We are rigorous and scientific. We make the tough assumptions that people are self-interested and calculating. We see people as autonomous, independent, and rational. We use precise math. We study markets, and perhaps	*We aren't* touchy-feely and humanistic. We don't make the sentimental assumption that people care about each other. We reject the idea that people could be connected, dependent, or emotional. We don't use

industry and government. We
describe mechanisms.

We're macho guys.

vague verbal arguments. We
don't study family life. We don't
deal with human relations or
ethics.

We're not soft, effeminate scholars,
like those sociologists and
humanists downstairs.

One way of interpreting this undercurrent, of course,
would be to buy into the idea that there is something natural and
right about all this. I might have concluded that economics really
is masculine and rational, while my experience as a female in an
interdependent family was noneconomic. I could have accepted
the split that has run through economics since the time of Smith.
I could have accepted the Victorian identification of economics
with self-interest, calculation, and men, and of "noneconomic"
life with ethics, care, and women.

But something felt wrong about this. For one thing, I found
it insulting to men to believe that they are inherently less moral
than women and implausible to believe that they have no emotional lives. For another, I knew from experience that rationality was not an exclusively Y-chromosome characteristic and that
women could act out of self-interest. And, as a woman, I thought
it both bizarre and unfair that all the characteristics and realms
of work traditionally associated with women should be so deni-
grated and ignored by the economics profession.

So I decided, instead, to question the whole mechanical
metaphor.

"But the economy really *is* mechanical," you might object.
"You keep saying 'mechanical metaphor' as if the comparison of
the economy to a machine is just some fancy flourish of speech,

instead of reflecting the deep, underlying structure of the world!"

I will reply to this objection on three levels. First, I will draw on the philosophy of language and science to show how metaphors work and why they are so important in scientific thought. This is the subject of the first section of this chapter. Second, once I have clarified the metaphorical nature of the idea that the economy is mechanical, I will move on to the question of whether this is a *useful* metaphor. I will begin to show how damaging this metaphor is, when held to exclusively, and suggest an alternative metaphor. Third, I will bring factual information to bear on some of the common misperceptions about economic life. This last part will be taken up in the following two chapters, where I will show that many common beliefs about the "mechanisms" and "forces" that drive economics are either vastly exaggerated or simply untrue.

Science and Metaphor

Science, in a general sense, is about sustained and systematic inquiry, as free of preconceptions and prejudgments as possible. Historians of science such as Thomas Kuhn have shown how the progress of science has often involved "paradigm shifts." That is, scientists tend to work with a given background of accepted knowledge—up to a point. Periodically, however, an accumulation of evidence that does not fit their existing general view forces them into a whole new way of looking at things.[1]

Metaphors are commonly the way in which a general worldview or understanding is expressed. "The essence of metaphor is understanding and experiencing one kind of thing in terms of another," claim linguist George Lakoff and philosopher Mark

Johnson, authors of *Metaphors We Live By*. According to them, and numerous other contemporary researchers in the areas of cognition, philosophy, rhetoric, and linguistics, metaphor is not merely a fancy addition to language. Instead, it is the fundamental way in which we understand our world and communicate our understanding from one person to another. Lakoff and Johnson give many examples of how the language we use reflects metaphorical elaborations of more abstract concepts on the foundation of basic physical experiences. Our perception of "up/down," for example, forms the basis for "good is up, bad is down," "reason is up, emotion is down," "control is up, subjection is down," and "high status is up, low status is down." Richer meanings can be found in more complex metaphors such as "argument is war" (reflected in language like "win," "lose," "defend," "attack") or "argument is a building" ("groundwork," "framework," "construct," "buttress," "fall apart"). [2]

These metaphors affect our understanding and our actions: for example, if we perceive ourselves as engaged in an argument, how we interpret what we hear and how we respond depends in good part on which metaphor we use. Metaphorical understanding is also culturally variable. For example, as Lakoff and Johnson suggest, there could exist another culture that uses the metaphor "argument is dance" and so uses a language of aesthetics, style, and synchronization in describing it. Metaphors illuminate some aspects of what they describe, while hiding others. They are never complete, literal descriptions.

Metaphors are also basic to science, since there is no way to describe something new except in terms of something with which we are already familiar. Light, for example, has been described both in terms of waves (like those on the sea) and in terms of particles (bits of matter apparent to our sight or touch). Neither metaphor is *literally* true, because both are incomplete. As I explained earlier, at the rise of modern science in the seventeenth century, the dominant metaphor was "the world is a machine," which had replaced the medieval understanding, "the world is a living being."

The clockwork metaphor that undergirded Newtonian mechanics has, however, long since been abandoned by scientists as an adequate metaphor for describing the whole physical world. The "laws of motion" that Newton laid out work reasonably well at describing force and movement at the level we experience in our daily lives. The movements of billiard balls, pendulums, and clocks can be closely predicted by his models and formulas. But when scientists began to look at very small or very large phenomena, the old metaphor became inadequate. The subatomic particles that make up atoms don't act like billiard balls. Black holes and the evolution of galaxies can't be explained using metaphors of gears and levers. The development of quantum theory, the theory of relativity, and the theory of complex systems has expanded physics far beyond the original Newtonian images and theories.

An open-minded approach to the evidence has meant abandoning the idea that the world is a machine. Some scientists now suggest that an atom is a "whirlpool of energy." Others suggest that "elementary particles are musical notes" created by the motion of "strings." Even the role played by mathematics has become somewhat more tenuous, as scientists are forced to question whether some complex aspects of the world can ever be described in formulas. A scientific practice that is worth its salt investigates the evidence and is willing to change metaphors and techniques when the need arises.

As I described in chapters 1 and 2, the metaphor of "the economy is a machine" arose in the eighteenth century based on the broader and earlier metaphor, "the world is a machine." While physical science has moved on, our popular and academic image of economies has remained firmly based in that seventeenth-century perception of the world. Why? Why do we persist in seeing the economy as an impersonal machine of particles and forces?

I believe that the image of the world as mechanical, and of scientists as its objective investigators and controllers, has a certain psychological appeal. I believe that, among economists, this appeal is a major force behind the persistence of the mechanical metaphor.

The psychological appeal of this image has an interesting history. A substantial literature developed during the 1980s about the rise of modern science, taking a new angle on the subject. Scholars such as Evelyn Fox Keller, Susan Bordo, Sandra Harding, and Brian Easlea pointed out that mind, reason, and objectivity were often linked with symbols of *masculinity* by many early scientists. These early leaders felt that the project of science was to give mind, reason, and objectivity dominion over the body, emotions, and subjectivity, which were characterized as alien and feminine.[3]

Henry Oldenburg, an early Secretary of the British Royal Society, for example, stated that the intent of the Society was to "raise a masculine Philosophy . . . whereby the Mind of Man may be ennobled with the knowledge of Solid Truths." James Hillman, in *The Myth of Analysis* writes, "The specific consciousness we call scientific, Western and modern is the long sharpened tool of the masculine mind that has discarded parts of its own substance, calling it 'Eve,' 'female' and 'inferior.'"[4]

The project of making and keeping economics "masculine" can thus be seen as part of a larger historical project of keeping "rational man" in charge—while keeping real bodies, needs, dependencies, and emotions carefully neutralized by labeling them "feminine" and thus easy to set aside. The mechanical metaphor fits the bill beautifully, keeping in economics only those characteristics that seem "tough" and rejecting all those that seem effeminate.

The really cheap part of this project, however, is that while Newton based his clockwork theories on *evidence* he gathered from experience, neoclassical economics bases its theories on *assumptions*. As I described in chapter 1, the early neoclassical economists were intent on making economics "scientific," by which they meant describing its "laws of motion." In other words, their goal was to make economics conform to the images and methods of Newtonian physics, which they mistook as representing science *in general*.

This overly narrow and rigid image of science has become economics' Procrustean bed. Complex human motivations didn't fit, so the discipline lopped them off. Relations of care— or of power, for that matter—didn't fit, so they went too. "Needs" dropped onto the slag pile. Only thin concepts of self-interest, profit, utility, and maximization survived. While Newton's theories fit certain phenomena well enough to be useful in explaining some parts of the physical world, no one even asked whether economists' theories fit the economic world they were supposed to be describing. Evidence that people act in their economic lives in ways contrary to the theory were, and continue to be, largely sloughed off, due to economists' desires to remain "rigorous" and "tough."

What kind of *science* is this, which holds to one metaphor unquestioningly and throws out all evidence that might require its practitioners to think anew?

Breaking Out of the Iron Cage

The "iron cage" described in chapter 2 is not out there in the world. It is in our heads, trapping our minds into a rigid way of thinking.

Smith, looking at the economy, theorized a fabulous machine of self-interest-motivated production and exchange. The neoclassicals theorized "firms" and "households" solving mathematical maximization problems and interacting at arm's length on perfectly functioning, abstract markets. Weber and Habermas theorized an economic system bereft of social meaning and human relationships. Such theories about "firms," "households," "the market," and "system vs. lifeworld" fit nicely onto a blackboard. But what do we see if we take our eyes off the board and actually look around us?

I see businesses that are complex organizations of people, styled along many different patterns of leadership and management. Some put a high priority on shareholder profits, while others seem more oriented toward growth, and still others seem to be run for the personal aggrandizement of their chief officers. Some businesses take their responsibilities to employees and communities seriously, while others do not. Some businesses run smoothly, while in others the right hand doesn't know what the left is doing. Some jump from one crisis to the next. Some create or promote technological and social innovations (like television advertising or Internet information and commerce) that profoundly change our lives. I can't see how one simple mathematical function can possibly begin to describe the role of businesses in economic life. The "maximize profits" idea is in our heads. Complex businesses really exist. (We will return to the definition of profits and factual issues related to business in chapter 5.)

Likewise, people in households act from a variety of motives and are organized in a variety of complex ways. People face real dilemmas in their choices about where to work, what to purchase, how to form their families, and how to participate in public decisions. Neoclassical theory extended to households would have us believe that parents trade off the "utility" they get from having children or voting to protect the environment with the "utility" they get from, say, eating ice cream, as if all household decisions were completely commensurable with each other. I do not see real people making their decisions that way. Neoclassical theory also treats the formation of people's preferences as outside its realm, taking whatever people want as "given." The role of advertising and social comparisons in influencing people's behavior is, rather amazingly, treated as not important to the understanding of economics. The "maximize utility" idea is in our heads. Complex households really exist.

Basic neoclassical theory neglects government and nongovernmental nonprofit organizations entirely. Labor unions, trade associations, church and charitable groups, and nonprofit hospitals and colleges play a tremendous role in the economic life of many communities. But they don't exist in the theory. Government spending on local and national security, and on health and education, has a huge impact on economic life, but government activity is portrayed as an awkward add-on to the "real" economy of firms and consumers. Neoliberals even accuse governments of "interfering" in otherwise perfectly running economic machines.

The theory pays no attention to the institutional requirements of markets. A real-world market needs institutions, both physical (like a shopping mall) and social (like the acceptability of credit cards) to function. The World Trade Organization seeks to set rules for international markets. Did you know that the New York Stock Exchange is itself a nonprofit institution? But actual market institutions are neglected in economics, in favor of abstract, blackboard images of purely impersonal, smooth, and rule-free exchange. "The Market" is in our heads. Complex, specific markets really exist.

As if that weren't enough, the image of the economy as a grand mechanical system of market exchange also neglects the role of transfers in economic life. By focusing only on exchange, the image neglects all the economic activity that involves a one-way transfer of money, goods, services, or assets for which nothing specific is expected in return. The goods and care transferred from parents to children are ignored. Taxes, subsidies, and government transfers for health and welfare are considered to be tangential to the real economy. (This is rather ironic, since, in fact, the first recorded use of monetary accounting was for the purpose of keeping track of taxes.) The role of inheritance in determining individuals' economic prospects is covered over. Charitable giving and the plunder of war are ignored.

The real economy is simply much larger and more complex than "firms" and "households" acting on markets. If we persist in thinking that the mechanical image describes the world, in defiance of the evidence, we fall into what mathematician and philosopher Alfred North Whitehead (1861–1947) called the "fallacy of misplaced concreteness." That is, sometimes we fall so in love with our abstractions that we come to think that they are more real than the world around us; we measure everything in terms of some Platonic ideal and see the actual world as simply a somewhat less than perfect manifestation of what we believe is going on "behind the scenes." If the world on stage doesn't correspond to our backstage mental image, we keep a tight grip on the mental image and chalk the differences in performance up to minor imperfections. But perhaps, instead, it is time to give up that background mental image of the economy as a machine.

When I look around me, the suitability of the machine metaphor is far from obvious. Economies involve people, in addition to cogs and wheels. Real human motivations, real human bodies and psychology, and real human decisions are behind economic action every step of the way.

What If the Economy Isn't a Machine?

The idea that the economy is a machine driven by self-interest could, of course, be accepted as metaphorical and still be considered to be the best base for coming up with practical economic policies. Or it could still be considered to be a relatively accurate way of delineating economic issues from moral issues. So we need to ask *why* it would be a good thing to drop the mechanical metaphor. Obviously, I need to show that dropping it would have good, real-world consequences.

Is the clockwork metaphor useful? In physics, the idea that the world is a machine made up of particles and forces describable by calculus has had considerable practical payoff. The mathematical elaboration of this idea within the physical sciences (even though it is false when taken generally) has contributed to the design of working toasters, space ships, and medical devices.

In economics, on the other hand, it is questionable how much all the mathematically sophisticated elaboration on this mechanical metaphor has contributed to anything of practical use. Most academic articles conclude with a "policy implications" section, but this is often strained and only rarely contributes to actual government and business discussions. Many of the most significant developments in economic policymaking, such as President Franklin Delano Roosevelt's New Deal, Keynesian activist macroeconomic policies, and Ronald Reagan's supply-side policies, had little or nothing to do with neoclassical economists' sophisticated application of calculus and statistics. The New Deal and Keynesian policies were direct responses to the *failure* of the "machine" to be as "self-regulating" as supposed. Supply-side policies were based on a graph scrawled on a napkin by minor-league economist Arthur Laffer, with no backing in mathematical modeling or empirical study whatsoever. Compared to the dramatic practical contributions of Newtonian physics, the "scientific" elaboration of the Newtonian paradigm in economics has been a dry well. One might say that its biggest contribution has been full employment—for neoclassical economists, that is, who have found a way to be paid to spend their time impressing each other with mathematical cleverness.[5]

Is the metaphor damaging? I believe it is. It has encouraged on the one hand the development of naive and irresponsible neoliberal probusiness policies, and on the other hand the development of naive and impractical antimarket alternatives.

Recall that in chapter 1, I attributed some pretty decent values, such as provisioning and job creation, to the probusiness camp. But I criticized them for claiming that the market system provides good things *automatically*, because it is a machine that needs no energy other than self-interest. In chapter 2, I pointed out that the market critics also prioritize valid values, such as moral development and concern for the needy. I criticized these market critics for claiming that the market, being a machine driven by self interest, is inimical to these values. The probusiness and antimarket groups are, ironically, blocked from dialogue with each other by their *common* assumption that the economy is a machine.

The schema shown in the figure opposite combines the four lists introduced in chapters 1 and 2. The positive values of the probusiness camp, List I, are reproduced in the top left box, representing a positive view about economics and the things we go through to make a living. The positive values of the market critics, List III, are reproduced in the top right box, representing a positive view about ethics and the things that make a life worth living.

The lower left box, containing List IV, reflects a negative view of economics, listing what antimarket advocates call "economic values," as I described earlier. The box on the lower right, containing List II, reflects probusiness advocates' negative view of antimarket folks as a bunch of useless (or worse), deluded do-gooders.

Here is the new point: I believe it is also the case that, because the economy is *not* a machine, both the probusiness and anti-market advocates have grasped only parts of the picture. By respecting the good things each side values, while dropping the idea that these good things are *automatically* either provided or destroyed by economic life, we can more adequately understand the relation of economics and ethics.

The List IV characteristics placed in the lower left box are the likely outcomes of a one-sided loyalty to economic life that demonstrates a *lack* of concern for issues of ethics and

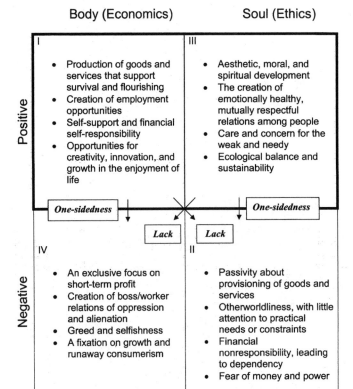

	Body (Economics)	Soul (Ethics)
Positive	**I** • Production of goods and services that support survival and flourishing • Creation of employment opportunities • Self-support and financial self-responsibility • Opportunities for creativity, innovation, and growth in the enjoyment of life	**III** • Aesthetic, moral, and spiritual development • The creation of emotionally healthy, mutually respectful relations among people • Care and concern for the weak and needy • Ecological balance and sustainability
Negative	**IV** • An exclusive focus on short-term profit • Creation of boss/worker relations of oppression and alienation • Greed and selfishness • A fixation on growth and runaway consumerism	**II** • Passivity about provisioning of goods and services • Otherworldliness, with little attention to practical needs or constraints • Financial nonresponsibility, leading to dependency • Fear of money and power

One-sidedness   *One-sidedness*   *Lack*   *Lack*

Probusiness advocates and antimarket critics each promote a collection of worthy virtues. Probusiness advocates emphasize values of bodily provisioning and self-reliance (List I), while critics of markets emphasize values of relationship, care, and sustainability (List III). But each side takes a one-sided view. Probusiness advocates, believing that economies are mechanical, decide that ethics are unnecessary. The outcome of their concern with "body" to the exclusion of a concern for "soul" is the vices in List IV. Antimarket critics, also believing that economies are mechanical, conclude that their ethical concerns can never be satisfied in capitalist economies. The outcome of their concern with "soul" to the neglect of "body" is the vices in List II. The shared belief that economies are mechanical keeps the two sides from recognizing that List I and List III are in fact compatible and complementary.

relationships. For example, producing goods *without* thinking about moral implications can easily lead to the marketing of harmful products. Creating jobs *without* respecting the humanity of the employees can easily lead to the creation of inhumane working conditions. A belief that everyone should be responsible for themselves *without* acknowledging the realities of human childhood, illness, and old age leads to an attitude of hard-heartedness. Producing or consuming products *without* paying attention to ecological impacts puts the earth's future in hock to the short-sighted impulses of the current generation. It isn't bad to want to create goods and jobs. But if you do so assuming that the ethical implications will "take care of themselves," you can cause real harm.

The List II characteristics placed in the lower right box are the likely outcomes of a one-sided loyalty to ethics that demonstrates a *lack* of concern for the practical provisioning of life. Being totally unconcerned about the provisioning side of life means, essentially, that you expect someone else to support you while you occupy yourself with "higher" things.[6] The Victorian lady who was supposed to be the defender of morals, for example, was also explicitly depicted as unconcerned with money, otherworldly and spiritual, and willing to put everyone else's needs ahead of her own. The Buddhist monk or nun, to take another example, even now in many Eastern countries devotes himself or herself to meditation and goes out once a day with a begging bowl to get food from neighboring farmers. I am not saying that "higher" things are not worthwhile. It may even be that withdrawal from the concerns of provisioning can be a good thing for some periods of time.

But consider two problems. First, we can't *all* take a one-sided ethics position. *Someone* has to pay attention to finances, bring home the bacon, pay the bills, or take the role of the farmer. Second, the ethics-only approach makes ethics *subject to* economic power. The degree to which the Victorian housewife or the Eastern monk or nun is able to continue to pursue her or his "higher" tasks is completely dictated by the whim of the people who provide support. Unless ethical work is more firmly tied to an economic base, the rug can be pulled out from under it at any moment. (Many divorced or abandoned housewives learned this to their great pain.) Ethics and care are very vulnerable when divorced from economics. We will look in more detail at the problems caused by this ungrounded ethics-only ideology in chapter 4.

What is exciting about the possibility of dropping the clockwork metaphor is that the top two boxes *can be recognized as complementary and valuable*. It is the machine metaphor, not life, that tells us that ethics are irrelevant to economics. It is the machine metaphor, not life, that tells us that "economic values" are limited to self-interest. If we listen to experience instead of to the stale metaphor, we can see that an active concern for ethics and an active concern for economic life are not only compatible, but depend on each other. We can leave neither side to automatism. We can take responsibility for provisioning *and* for care. We can take active responsibility for the entire socioeconomic system in which we participate and which sustains us. We can bring body and soul back together.

The Beating Heart

Stop, look, and listen. The rhythm you hear is not the ticking of the economic clock, but the beating of the economic heart.

Metaphors are powerful. No matter how subtle and sophisticated we would like to believe we are in our thinking, basic visual or tactile images create the very foundations of our thought. The image of the mechanical gears of the ticking economic clock—powered by self-interest, capable of perpetual motion, eternally functioning according to a predesigned, behind-the-scenes blueprint, and subject only to tinkering by mathematics-educated econo-engineers—is a concrete and graspable image that has held mighty sway.

Among the many alternative metaphors that could be imagined for economic life, the metaphor of "the economy as a beating heart" seems to me to be particularly apt.[7] On the one hand, many of the associations that come from visualizing a heart as a vital bodily *organ of circulation* can be easily recognized as appropriate for describing economies. The heart moves flows of lifeblood throughout the body. Economies have often, likewise, been visualized in terms of circular flows, keeping money, goods, and services on the move. The heart has a particular physical structure (valves and chambers) and regularity of functioning. Imagining the economy as a heart recognizes that it also has structures (institutions) and regularities. Thus far, the metaphor only calls on characteristics that might also be drawn from traditional analogies relating both economies and hearts to pumping machines.

But because the heart is a living, *vital* organ—not an inanimate pumping machine—additional highly relevant insights flow from this metaphor. A beating heart is essential for the life of an individual body, creating the flow that carries oxygen and nutrients to the body's cells. Likewise, an economy creates the flow of provisions that sustain and enrich the lives of individuals and society. As a living entity, the economic heart can be kept healthy and strong, or it can become weak, clogged, and degenerate. When money and goods do not circulate, but rather build up in unhealthy concentrations, an economy can be said to be in danger of congestive "heart" failure. Any part of the economic body that is cut off from the provisioning flow withers and dies. As a living entity, economic hearts adapt and coevolve with the culture, history, ecology, and institutions that surround them. Just as the heart of a bird differs from the heart of a mammal, there is no one-size-fits-all economy.[8] Economic hearts can bleed, when conflicts and power struggles over access to economic goods leads to the shedding of (literal or metaphorical) blood. A heart requires energy and nutrients that come from outside itself—ultimately, from the ecological environment. A sick or injured heart requires treatment by examination, diagnosis, and care. As a living thing, a heart that gets too ill or injured, or can no longer get the resources it needs, can die.

The heart is also the *center of love*. It is, as illustrated by many myths and stories, the seat of care and compassion. From its stylized ubiquity on Valentine's Day cards to the slogan of "have a heart" in charity campaigns, the heart symbolizes our deep attachments to one another. The heart is also the symbolic center of integrity and conscience, as when one says, "I knew in my heart it was wrong." In some Eastern cultures, bowing with your hands pressed together over your heart is a symbol of respect—of recognition that the other person carries a spark of the divine within.

The image of the economy as a beating heart, then, can be simultaneously a symbol of bodily provisioning *and* a symbol of care, respect, and moral and spiritual life. The heart's existence as a physical organ brings out the "body" side of the schema, while its cultural symbolism as the seat of love evokes the "soul" side.

Lastly, the heart is also the seat of motivation and *courage*. To "not have the heart for something" is not to be able to pull yourself together to do it. The Cowardly Lion in *The Wizard of Oz* asked for a heart to give him fortitude. In the clockwork image of economies, we don't need courage because we are simply cogs in the machine—we can say "the system made me do it." In the heart of economics, on the other hand, we need all the courage we can get. We need it because we are obliged to take responsibility for our actions. The image of the economy as a beating heart not only brings together body and soul, but points us toward action regarding the heartaches of poverty, hunger, injustice, empty consumerism, and ecological destruction. With no machine to do the job of alleviating these for us, it is *our* job to see that economies become vital and caring. Weak hearts will not be adequate to the task.[9]

Economics and Responsibility

There are many excellent people, of course, already doing authentic and valuable work in the fields of spirituality in the workplace, human relations within organizations, business ethics, corporate social responsibility, the financing and organization of caring work, and other projects that bring ethics and economics together. Many caring, courageous people are concerned with creating and preserving a healthy, vital economic life and are already on the job. I don't need to reinvent their fields.

But the probusiness zealots I've described *don't listen* to what any of these people have to say, because they believe that the Smithian machine works just fine without ethical "obstructions." As conservative economist Milton Friedman has famously asserted, "Few trends could so thoroughly undermine the very foundations of our free society as the acceptance by corporate officials of a social responsibility other than to make as much money for their stockholders as possible."[10] In this view, a business that pays attention to the human needs of its employees, employees' families, clients, or communities is actually seen as *ir*responsible!

Antimarket pundits *don't listen* either, because they are sure that "corporate social responsibility" is a contradiction in terms. David Korten, for example, voices the view of many when he dismisses ethical-seeming behaviors on the part of large corporations as merely shallow public relations ploys.[11] Many who want to protect "noneconomic values" in areas of health and education take it as bedrock truth that economics equals greed.

I hope that by reaching back into the seventeenth century and examining the economy-as-machine metaphor at its roots, I have helped to remove one obstacle to serious discussion of the ethics of contemporary economic life. The hold of the clockwork metaphor has been one important factor blocking dialogue and useful action. With the metaphor called into serious question, "business ethics" and "the economics of care" seem less like oxymorons. Adopting the metaphor of the *economy as a beating heart* takes us even further. To remain healthy, our economic life must be vital, caring, and responsible. "Business ethics" and "the economics of care" are not just options but *requirements*.

But there are still factual matters to address, on two levels. The first level is that of individual motivation and interpersonal relations. Doesn't an individual doing something "for the money" mean that he or she lacks other, more tender, motivations? Or doesn't working "for pay" put an employee under the thumb of his or her employer? This is the subject of the next chapter. The second level is that of organizations and their relations to the world outside them. Aren't corporations *forced* to maximize profits, by legal mandates or market forces, at the expense of all other concerns? This is the subject of chapter 5.

4

LOVE *AND* MONEY?

The Question of Individual Motivation

A Dilemma in Care

Rosa Hernandez is a lower-working-class mother of two children and foster mother of two more. Asked about the two-year-old foster child who has been with her since birth, she says,

> It will break my heart when he is adopted. There is no way
> you can't get attached if you're supposed to love them and
> nurture them and give them a good home. But then [case-
> workers and lawyers] turn around and say if you can't
> adopt them then we'll take them; you must not really care
> about him after all. But we can't afford it; we would lose his
> MediCal, and he has asthma. We might lose everything;
> then we couldn't take care of anybody.

Teresa Toguchi Swartz, the sociologist who noted down Ms. Hernandez's thoughts, also interviewed the social service professionals that supervise the foster parents. "The caseworkers and lawyers," she found, accused Rosa and her husband "of fostering only for the money and not truly caring about the boys if they did not adopt."[1] What's going on here? Ms. Hernandez is working from an attitude of economic *and* ethical responsibility. She and her husband, a $1,000 per month dockworker, take seriously their responsibility to support their family. They also take seriously the relation of love and intimacy they have established with the little boy. In terms of the lists and schema introduced earlier, these foster parents value *both* List I and List III and see love and money as *complementary*. The boy's medical coverage monies support them in continuing to care for him. But they will lose access to those funds if they adopt.

The social service professionals, on the other hand, are taking an ethics-only, antimoney view. They see Ms. Hernandez's interest in money as a signal that she must not really care about the boy himself. They are so concerned about the nonfinancial aspects of care for the boy that they completely overlook the practical needs and constraints facing the Hernandez family. They probably think of themselves as List III people—concerned with the weak and needy. I say that they are List II people—so concerned with "higher things" that they have become otherworldly and blind to the financial realities facing a working-class family. They are so high-minded that they are prepared to wrest a boy from the people whom he loves and who love him.[2]

It comes down to a question of motivation. Can a person be motivated by love and at the same time be motivated by money? Many people say "no." They believe that anything done for money automatically becomes "commodified." They identify transactions that involve money with narrow self-interested calculation. They believe that a worker's willingness to accept little reimbursement for caring work is a sign that he or she is appropriately compassionate.[3] The topic of motivations and care is the first one I will take up in this chapter.

A more general but closely related question concerns motivations in the case where we already expect that people *are* motivated by money. When people work "for pay" in, say, a modern corporation, does that mean they have handed over their will to the boss? Or are other motivations still important there, as well?

These are two sides of the same coin: Can you work "for money" in an occupation that, by its nature, clearly calls on your capacity to love? Can you have love in your work, perhaps in an office or factory, given that the main reason you engage in it is "for money"?

The Historical Legacy

Historically, of course, caring work *was* nonmarket work, and market work was culturally portrayed as being by its nature harsh and noncaring. The love-versus-money ideology fit hand-in-glove with the prevailing social arrangements in middle-class households.

As I mentioned earlier, in Victorian times economic life in the marketplace was thought of as cold, harsh, and mechanical. Middle-class men, brutalized by their days of competitive deal-making, would, it was thought, need a haven to return to at the end of the day. The home, idealized as a realm of warmth, high moral values, and feminine arts, was thought to provide this haven for individual men and also a spiritual and civilizing counterbalance for society as a whole.

The care given to children, the sick, and the elderly by middle-class women in their homes was only *indirectly* economically supported, via the support the woman herself received from her husband. Because relations between spouses were largely thought of—in both popular culture and law—as mutual gift-giving (as opposed to "crass" exchange), what women did at home was not considered to be "work." Women were considered to be the economic dependents of their husbands. The time and money resources that actually went into caring, then, were well-insulated from any clear connection to finance or markets.

While Victorian ideology is propounded today by some groups, it was never really an accurate description of economic life. Except for a small elite, women who did not work for pay still *worked*. They made substantial economic contributions, provisioning their families with cooking, cleaning, and care. And many more women who did not have middle-class husbands dealt directly with the harshest parts of the industrial economy. Sweatshops and factories employed minority, immigrant, and poor women. Their young children often worked right beside them, for long hours and for low pay. The middle-class ideology of the Victorian "angel in the house" masked the work of running a home and glossed over the effects of industrialization on poor women and children.

Even when caring work began increasingly to move out of the household, the idea that carework was not serious income-earning work persisted. Early nurses were often nuns who had taken vows of poverty. Other nurses were young women who took on nursing as a temporary occupation until they could get married. Neither needed to be paid much, being that they had no dependents and could expect their overall welfare to be taken care of by their religious orders, their fathers, or their future husbands. Early nursery schools and day care centers were often begun and staffed by married, middle-class church women as charity directed toward women and children of lesser privilege. These women could be paid little—"pin money," it was sometimes called—because their husbands had "breadwinner" jobs. Primary teaching likewise came to be dominated by the likes of nuns, young single women, and married women with employed husbands. The economic support of care continued to come only indirectly, through family or religious support, rather than directly to the care worker.

The Victorian ideology of caring home versus cold factory still often resonates with us because we feel there is a qualitative aspect to motivations for care that is absent (or less pronounced) in other types of work. The very nature of carework rests on a personal, emotional concern for the dependent person. Nurses, health aides, child care workers, and foster parents, we hope, are sincerely concerned about the well-being of the people they assist and nurture. We certainly don't want people doing these jobs who are thinking only about their own paychecks. We don't want grandma in the nursing home or our child at day care being handled roughly and coldly by someone who measures their job only in terms of the number of shots administered or diapers changed. We rightly fear carework taking on what we think of as an industrial, assembly-line mentality. We want to make sure there is some heart involved.

The historical legacy of Victorian attitudes, however, has left us with a tendency to consider only false alternatives. Either the work is done coldly "for the money," we tend to think, or it is done "freely," for love. We tend to have an idea that genuine care should just emerge from nature like an inexhaustible spring.

Times have changed. A big pool of women used to be available for carework because everything else was closed off to them. Now professions beyond nursing and teaching are open to women. A big pool of women used to be able to work for low or no wages because they were otherwise supported. Now single-parent households and dual-career households are much more prevalent than they used to be. These days, child care centers, nursing homes, and home health agencies complain that they can't find anywhere near enough good workers. Hospitals seem to be battling a never-ending shortage of nurses. School districts face a dearth of teachers. The spring of care doesn't seem so inexhaustible anymore.

Consider this problem of a shortage of workers for a moment. What do employers *generally* do when they can't find the number of workers they need? If employers can't find enough assembly-line workers, salespeople, or engineers, what do they do? These jobs do not have a large, explicit personal care component, and we generally accept that people do these jobs "for money." Of course. We have assumed, since the time of Adam Smith, that people are self-interested in their economic life. If a company needs more assembly-line workers, salespeople, or engineers than it can get at the financial compensation it is offering, it commonly increases the wages or perks that it offers.

Some people argue that raising wages to try to get more care workers, as a company might do to get more engineers, would be a *bad* policy. It would attract the wrong kind of people, they say. High compensation would attract people doing the job just "for pay." Presumably these money-motivated people would put on only a show of superficial caring sufficient to keep the money coming. Raises are hence rarely suggested as a tool for recruiting or retaining care workers, even in the face of persistent shortages. People afraid of contaminating care with "economic values" believe they *protect* caring work by keeping it low paid.

But is this presumed opposition between caring and monetary motivations a fact, or are we just stuck in outdated ways of thinking?

What Research Says about Love and Money

People who want to argue that money drives out care and concern can turn to parts of philosophy and the social sciences for apparent support. Jürgen Habermas, whose work on "lifeworld" versus "system" I introduced in chapter 2, would be one advocate of this view. Recall that he believes that the media of money "drives" the economic system. Whenever impersonal money enters the scene, he believes, activities are "technicized" and drained of human and social meaning.

Money, in Habermas's view, really has a life and force of its own. He has claimed that it is backed up by "gold or means of enforcement," and therefore its use does not require social legitimation.[4] He believes it exists as an objective reality, outside of social life, obeying rules that have nothing to do with social relations.

But let's examine this claim. What is money, really? Many people besides Habermas still think of a dollar bill as a certificate that represents a bit of a gold ingot at Fort Knox. But, in fact, money these days is *entirely* a social creation! The international gold standard collapsed in the early 1930s and all idea of dollar convertibility to gold was completely abandoned in 1971.

Those economists who take money seriously are *very* aware that money is useful in exchange exactly to the extent that its users *agree* that it has value. There is no outside "enforcement" for the value of national currencies. One of the main functions of national central banks is to take actions to keep the national currency *legitimate* in the eyes of its users. Central banks are constantly trying *to assure* people that their dollars, pesos, or Euros can be trusted to remain acceptable in trade and as a store of value. Leaders of central banks worry about beliefs, expectations, credibility, reputation, legitimacy, and the problems of collective decision making—not about the quantity of gold in a vault somewhere.[5] Some of the major international upheavals in recent economic history have been directly due to crises of legitimation, sparked when expectations of hyperinflation or massive devaluation led to a public lack of confidence in a currency's value. Money is not backed by gold or enforcement. It is very much a social creation.

Because the meaning of money depends entirely on social beliefs, Habermas's argument about money as a destroyer of social meaning doesn't make sense. But perhaps social science research says there is something about the interaction of money and human motivations that causes money to drive out care?

Richard Titmuss's comparative study of the human blood supply in the United States and Britain is often cited as evidence that money motivations and caring motivations are completely at odds with each other.[6] Britain, at the time of his study, relied on voluntary donors for its blood supply, while the United States relied on both voluntary donors and paid donors. Titmuss found that the U.S. system supplied blood of lower quality and at a higher cost than the British system. He suggested that having a commercial market for blood reduced people's willingness to donate blood voluntarily. Having one's charitable impulses put in direct juxtaposition with a monetary transaction, it seems, demeans and commodifies the activity. Titmuss's finding has often been interpreted broadly to mean that "gift" relationships motivated by care and concern are entirely different animals from "exchange" relationships motivated by money. Or, put another way, his findings have been said to prove that money motivations "crowd out" caring motivations.

This is only half the story, however. Bruno Frey is an economist who has intensively studied the relations of money and motivations. He has, like Titmuss, concluded that "external interventions" such as a money payment can "*crowd-out* intrinsic motivation" arising from care, ethics, loyalty, or enjoyment of the activity. But he found that this happens in *a particular social context*.[7] Money payments tend to crowd out intrinsic motivations when "they are perceived to be *controlling*." That is, when people feel that have to hand over control of their actions to someone else in order to receive payment for them, their internal motivations tend to be dampened and perhaps extinguished. Suppose, for example, a person chooses a career in counseling because he likes helping people. Suppose the organization he works for, however, makes him follow so many rigid routines and file so much paperwork that he feels constantly hemmed in and treated with suspicion. Put into an organization that treats him like a cog in a machine, he may very well eventually come to work "just for the money."

On the other hand, however, Frey found that if money payments "are perceived to be *acknowledging*," they can "*crowd-in* intrinsic motivation." If money payments acknowledge and support the worker's own goals and desires, then they *reinforce and magnify* the worker's interior motivations and satisfaction. People like feeling supported and recognized in their work, and monetary payment can be one way of expressing such support and recognition. Counselors, for example, who perceive that their organizations respect their work, and back up that respect with money, enjoy a morale boost that reinforces their confidence in their ability to help people. Getting a raise and respect is *heart*ening. I don't believe I've ever heard of a Nobel Prize winner turning down the money involved because she thought it would be "demeaning" to accept it!

In my own family, I've seen up close a case of how a "controlling" style of management can drive out care, while "acknowledging" management can support it. My oldest sister almost gave up nursing after many years of feeling exploited, unappreciated, and pushed around at her job at a large hospital. Schedules were handed down from above, and meager raises were granted by an administration that seemed indifferent, if not outright hostile, to the well-being of its nursing workforce (and sometimes its patients as well). Feeling disrespected and overcontrolled, she eventually barely dragged herself to the job "just for the money." After she moved to another, smaller, hospital, however, she realized that it had been bad management, not nursing, that had exhausted her. At the new hospital, she and the others in her work group are treated like responsible adults and allowed to work out their own schedules. My sister's jaw almost hit the floor one afternoon when she opened a letter from her new employer. The management, after reviewing the results of a study of local nursing wages, had decided to give all the nurses unplanned and unasked-for raises! She is again satisfied with her career choice. She feels respected for the caring work she does *and* makes good money.

Thus, it is not money itself that "drives out" caring feelings, but rather the social meaning given to the particular movement of money. Being motivated at least in part by money is *not* intrinsically opposed to motivation by care or other concerns! The beating heart of a healthy economy circulates money without "crowding out" people's desire to be caring and responsible.

Economic Motives

Let's take an even closer look at the relation of economics, money, and selfishness. "Economic motives" have so long been identified with financial self-interest and even greed that it is worth stopping to ask what we mean when we say people are "economically" motivated.

The first thing to notice is that even in the most obviously "economic" situations, people do not act out of solely financial interest. Economic behavior is not just about getting money. The second point to notice is that even when money is playing a large role in economic behavior, this need not mean that a person is greedy. Money-motivated behavior is not always selfish.

Economic Behavior Isn't Just about Getting Money

An interesting economic experiment has recently drawn considerable attention in the social sciences. In the "Ultimatum Game," two people are told they will be given a sum of money, say $20, to share. One person gets to propose a way of splitting the sum. For example, this first person may offer to share $10 with the second person, or only $8 or $1, and plan to keep the rest. The second person can't offer any input to this decision but gets to decide whether to accept the offer or reject it. If the second person rejects the offer, both people will walk away empty-handed. If the offer is accepted, they get the money and split it as planned. If the two people act only from narrow financial self-interest, then the first person should offer the second person the smallest possible amount—say $1—in order to keep the most for herself. The second person should accept this offer because, from the point of view of pure financial self-interest, $1 is better than nothing.

In fact, researchers find that deals that vary too far from a 50/50 split tend to be rejected. People would rather walk away with nothing than be treated in a way they perceive to be unfair!

Economic relations always take place within a social context, and because of this it is misleading to think that people's economic behavior is guided only by their individual financial interests. Social theorist Howard Margolis has suggested that rather than being motivated by pure self-interest, most people aspire to be "neither selfish nor exploited."[8] That is, people are generally willing to be helpful, cooperative, and contribute to the common good, at least up to a point. In a well-functioning society, most people, for example, refrain from stealing and pay their taxes even when the chance of being caught breaking the law is low. People even contribute money to charities. The turning point is reached when people feel that they are doing more than their share and that other people are taking advantage of them. Like the second person in the Ultimatum Game, people can become uncooperative and even vengeful if they feel they are not being treated with the dignity that is due them. If people perceive themselves to be in a society where other people steal and cheat and keep their goodies to themselves, they will be more likely to also steal, cheat, and hoard—to avoid becoming chumps. If people perceive themselves to be in a society of decent folks who are generally willing to be honest and carry their share of the load, they will also be generally honest and willing to carry their share of the load.

Think about this for a minute. Because our actual economic behavior is very much influenced by our social perceptions and beliefs, what we believe about economic life has the potential of becoming a self-fulfilling prophecy. If we propagate the machine-myth that people in their economic life are always simply on the lookout for their financial self-interest, which behavior do we encourage? Do we encourage generous behavior in the common interest, or an attitude of defensive self-protection?

Money-Motivated Behavior Is Not Always Selfish

People *need* money—for rent, for clothes, for the needs of their own families and children. Real people have real responsibilities. In a modern economy, people need to participate in the money economy in order to provide for themselves and others. Rosa Hernandez, the foster mother, understands this even if the middle-class social service professionals she deals with do not. She *really cares* about the boy in her care. But time spent caring for him, taking him to doctor's appointments for his asthma and the like, is time she can't *also* use to earn money in a factory or office. If she is to spend her time caring for the boy, this care has to be financially supported some way or other.

Sometimes people flip the equation of money and selfishness to its converse, and assume that being willing to take a job at *low* wages is a *sign* of being caring and compassionate. They imagine that people who are compassionate must be willing to "freely" offer their services, and they believe that truly caring people should be indifferent about their level of monetary compensation.

Surveys of child care workers and low-paid health aides, however, reveal that they are well aware of how badly they are paid relative to those in other occupations and that this is one of the reasons job turnover is so high. In one study, more than half the child care workers and directors interviewed expressed the sentiment, "I love my job but I'm about to leave it."[9] Many workers feel genuine care for their young or ill clients and find satisfaction in their work, but eventually they also feel forced to move to something more lucrative. (These days, one can make more money as a parking lot attendant than working in child care.) They may be able to stay in a caring job until a divorce, the birth of a child, or some other life event forces them to take on greater financial responsibilities. Or they may leave because they get tired of feeling undervalued, both economically and socially.

The sense of being exploited in caring work is especially intense for people who are more educated and skilled, and hence have attractive alternatives open to them. Many of the best folks end up leaving caring work for jobs with higher pay and social status, because they get tired of being poor and because they *can* leave. In the presence of real personal and family responsibilities, you have to notice that many people who would make excellent caregivers literally can't afford to stay in the job if it pays too little.

If people with attractive alternatives often tend to leave low-paid caring professions, who stays behind? Sometimes these are truly caring people who can afford the financial sacrifice because they are supported by other family members or have no dependents of their own. But, besides altruism, another reason a person may accept a low wage is because he *has no other alternatives.* Anecdotal evidence in the United States suggests that people employed as low-paid health aides, child care aides, foster parents, and the like include some very uneducated and low-skilled people, sometimes with addictions or criminal backgrounds. Because the physical tasks listed in the job descriptions call for little more than basic life skills, basic carework currently attracts and retains many people who would have a hard time finding a job anywhere else. They may or may not feel any genuine concern about the people they are hired to help. These days, the person taking care of your child or your grandmother may be doing it only because they didn't quite qualify for a job at McDonald's. We'd like to believe otherwise, but that is the hard reality when caring jobs are among the worst paid in the economy.

Certainly, we want people in caring jobs to *really care*. A low wage is no guarantee, however, that a worker will act out of true concern. Because of personal responsibilities and the attractiveness of alternative jobs, neither would higher wages necessarily disproportionately attract people to the field "just for the money." Higher wages could make it possible for caring people (that is, people who feel real concern) to care (that is, devote time to the activity of providing care). The best way to ensure the quality of care, then, is not to keep the wages low in order to attract (presumably) only people with a bent toward self-sacrifice. The best way to get real carers is to offer a level of economic support that *broadens the pool* of candidates and keeps people feeling *appropriately recognized and rewarded* in their work. The people running nursing homes, child care centers, and social service agencies and the like could then "cream" off the best candidates! The workers who prove to be the most sensitive and caring in interviews and on the job would get the work, at a wage that would keep them feeling good about what they are doing. Good wages would encourage workers to stay on the job, building the long-term personal relations that promote real human development and healing.

Exploitation

Rather than thinking about love *versus* money, we can think about love *and* money. In fact, if we really want high levels of love and care in our society, we need to be ready to *support* this goal with time and money. Continuing to think about economics as somehow opposed to caring and ethical behavior simply keeps care in a vulnerable, subordinated position.

Nurses, for example, are hampered in making a strong protest about problems of understaffing and unfairly low pay by this cultural association of economic interest with selfishness. In occupations that don't involve care, workers who are really fed up can simply walk off the job. Nurses and other caring workers, however, find it hard to refuse overtime, much less go on strike, because of the deeply embedded professional ethic that one simply *does not* walk away from a helpless patient or child, unless someone else is there to take over. They are to some extent, as feminist economist Nancy Folbre has termed it, "prisoners of love."[10]

Management knows this. Attempts by caring workers to improve the situation for themselves and those in their care can thus be hampered by management's strategic manipulation of the "love versus money" theme. In the city of Brockton, Massachusetts, for example, nurses went on strike in 2001, after careful planning to minimize the disruption to necessary care. Key negotiation points included issues of staffing, forced overtime, inappropriate floating, and pay. That is, the hospital had dealt with the nursing shortage by increasing pressure on existing nurses and downgrading the quality of care given to patients. Nurses were being forced to care for too many patients, to work when overtired and at unexpected times, and to "float" to jobs in areas of the hospital where they had little expertise.

How did the hospital respond? It played on all the old "love versus money" stereotypes. The *Boston Globe* reported, "Hospital executives said the nurses' true motive was to extract higher wages." That is, the hospital tried to communicate to the public, "There go those *selfish* nurses. You wouldn't want to support *selfish* nurses, would you?" The nurses, according to the hospital executives, also want to "advance their legislative agenda." Meddling in politics is presumably unnurselike. And, to twist the knife a little deeper: "Hospital vice president Robert Hughes said the union . . . walked out without waiting for a response. 'I'm actually quite appalled by it,' he said." To people who define their identities in large part in terms of connection and care, accusations of being rude and unwilling to communicate are designed to strike close to the heart.[11]

Could you imagine, say, steelworkers being subject to such rhetorical attack, even if their strike was explicitly about raising wages? I can't. All other people in the world—besides caregivers—are *expected* to be concerned with their own and their families' well-being. But to the extent that discussion of economics and politics is considered to somehow degrade "real" care, the ultimate result is that caring occupations are starved of resources and caregivers are exploited.

Working for a Buck

Now let's turn to another topic and consider those occupations where we assume that people work primarily "for the money." We don't necessarily expect that the assembly-line worker, salesperson, or engineer brings a lot of his or her emotional life to the job. The impersonal, clockwork idea of economic life appears at least superficially plausible here.

The simple, conventional story is that people get their jobs in the "labor market," which is just another place where something is exchanged for money. Workers enter into agreements with their employers to hand over their services in exchange for a wage. The process is unemotional and all transactions are made at arm's length. The simple story assumes that the payment of a wage puts an employee's action under the absolute control of the company, either directly or through hierarchical layers of management. The owners or shareholders of a business are assumed to be the ultimate directors of every worker's activities. In fact, in the late nineteenth and early twentieth centuries, the teachings of Taylorism, Fordism, and the rigid, controlling "scientific management" school encouraged companies to think about employees as just another kind of tool or machine.

To the probusiness advocates, this is all to the good. The invisible hand of markets coordinates these employment situations to yield the highest efficiency and greatest social good. Businesses need not be directly concerned with the well-being of their workers, according to this story. If they concentrate on profit, the rest will automatically fall into place, they believe.

To those who take an antimarket view, the employment relation is a sign of the intrinsically alienating nature of capitalism. Workers are separated from the product of their hands and minds by the capitalist wage relation, they say. Sociologist Julia O'Connell Davidson repeats the usual mechanistic view when she portrays the employer/employee relation under capitalism as a relation of domination between "those who pay others to do their will" and "those who get paid to surrender their own will."[12]

But is the *conventional story* at all accurate? Is the relation between an employee and his or her workplace simply one of a market exchange of money in return for unquestioning service?

Once we look *inside* the firm, there is a contradiction within the simple story that even some contemporary neoclassical labor economists have noted. Classical economist John Stuart Mill had said that people want to get what they want using "the smallest quantity of labour and physical self-denial" possible. But if this is true, it creates problems. Although people may have signed on to work for the good of a business, doesn't Mill's theory imply that, once hired, they will then tend to shirk whenever they are not being closely watched?

If dogged loyalty to the interest of the business can't be directly bought, then some other way of motivating people must be found. A business may try to keep people in line by having supervisors hanging over them every minute. A business might try to motivate production workers by paying them on a piece-rate basis and hire inspectors to check on the quality of the goods produced. A corporation may try to motivate an executive by way of stock options or other contract terms and hire auditors to make sure the executive doesn't cheat (à la Enron). But supervisors and inspectors and auditors are expensive—and someone has to be paid to keep *them* in line, too. Trying to manage a business using only extrinsic rewards and punishments can be a very expensive proposition.

It may also be ineffective, relative to alternatives. As I noted above, people can be motivated in their economic dealings by both extrinsic and intrinsic motivations. They want to get rewards (like pay) and avoid punishments (like being fired). But they also want to feel good about what they are doing and how they are being treated. Maybe John Stuart Mill was wrong. Maybe people will be willing to expend more effort if they feel loyalty to their employer, pride in their job, or joy in the relationships they have with coworkers. Maybe instead of treating employees merely like cogs and wheels and trying to control their every move, an employer could be better off treating employees like human beings, acknowledging their dignity and their social and emotional needs.

This intuition is confirmed by generous evidence on employee behavior. Many scholars of business, personnel management, and organizations discovered long ago that people do not simply leave their needs for social relations, their values, their loyalties, and their creativity at the workplace door. Many researchers have found that businesses may even be more successful when they rely relatively less on hierarchy and control and more on organizing the workplace around people's needs as social and emotional beings. Business scholars James C. Collins and Jerry I. Porras, for example, studied a number of businesses that had been unusually successful over time and concluded that attention to values was one of their key features: "People still have a fundamental human need to belong to something they can feel proud of. They have a fundamental need for guiding values and sense of purpose . . . a fundamental need for connection with other people. . . . [E]mployees will demand operating autonomy while also demanding that the organization they're connected to *stand* for something."[13] Many managers and researchers in organizational behavior share the insight that people work better when they are supported, empowered, and allowed to draw on their own creativity, than when they are consistently treated as potential shirkers who have to be brought under control. People want to be treated as real human beings. They want to have their unique interests and skills respected and at the same time to be connected with something bigger—and worthy of their efforts and their loyalty.

Even the worker on the assembly line may work better when he takes pride in what he produces and perceives that the company responds to workers' concerns about job pacing, hours, and time off for family needs. The salesperson or engineer may not be explicitly motivated by emotions of care, but her emotions of loyalty and pride in her work play a crucial role in what she does. I no more want my child to cross a bridge designed by an engineer who doesn't much care about the quality of her work than I want my child taught by a teacher who doesn't much care about his students.

A true cynic might say that an employment system which takes into account employees' social needs and values is even worse than a purely wage-oriented system. They might say that the employer is now not only controlling an employee's external activities, but also exploiting and manipulating his or her emotions. I have no doubt that in some cases this is true. I, too, have sat through meaningless retreats where "excellence" and "values" have been promoted by people who clearly do not really have anyone's interests at heart but their own. But I don't think that such efforts *always* have to be insincere.

The mechanical view of economic life simply does not have room for such things as loyalty, sincerity, or respect within relations of power. Discussions in philosophy and the social sciences based on the mechanical view hence function with a very limited range of possibilities concerning human relationships. Relations are, in fact, pretty much limited to only two extreme types. First, relationships can be arm's length. Such relationships are cool and contractual and relatively egalitarian as concerns the legal rights of each party. Conventional economists assume that this kind of relationship characterizes interactions in markets. Political theorists assume something similar when they hold up as an ideal an image of a purely democratic state or workplace in which everyone has exactly equal power and resources. The second possibility within the mechanical view is that of hierarchical relationship. In a hierarchy, the person with less power and resources takes a submissive position relative to the person with more power. The political theorists who believe that workers under capitalism are inherently alienated believe that boss/worker relations are inevitably characterized by disrespect for the weaker party. In both the arm's-length and hierarchical cases, the quality of the relation is measured only according to its external, power-differential characteristics—as it would be if we were talking about the forces going on within a machine. To many market-critic political theorists, the only alternatives for workplace life are either a strict democracy of power (such as in an idealized worker-managed firm) or a crushing hierarchy (under capitalism).

Only when we go beyond the mechanical view can we pay attention to a relationship's emotional content and *the qualitative way in which power is being used*. And here the previous discussion about money and caring work can help us envision new possibilities. In the relationship between a preschool teacher and a child, for example, the teacher has more power than the student. The teacher manages the course of the day. Likewise, in the relationship between a nurse and a very sick patient, the nurse has more power, giving (or withholding) the shots. When these relationships are healthy, however, the power these caregivers wield is *not* power of the sort described as domination or control. We don't (at least in the best cases) think of children or patients as mere submissive tools under the manipulation of teachers or nurses. In these relationships, we recognize the role of appropriate assignments of power within a mutual project directed toward nurturing or health. We know that there are good reasons for not letting the child decide when to cross the street, for not giving the patient unlimited access to morphine.

The relations in these cases are *not* characterized by strict equality of power, but they *are* characterized by respect and heart.

Now what about work groups in business and industry? Can we think about the possibility of having appropriate assignments of power, among human beings in all their dignity, within other kinds of mutual projects? People who lead work groups certainly have to pay attention to whether instrumental tasks of preparing a sales campaign or designing a bridge are being accomplished. They sometimes have to make decisions that are not what everyone under their direction would want. But this doesn't mean that leaders don't bring with them their own emotional and relational capabilities—their own hearts. It doesn't mean they can simply order people about and expect the job to be done well. Good management, much business research increasingly suggests, requires "soft skills" for dealing with the emotional and social aspects of getting a job done, as well as "hard skills" such as those involving finances and analysis. Envisioning relationships as *human* relationships, between people of flesh and blood, rather than looking at them purely from the viewpoint of the mechanical metaphor, opens up the possibility that work relations of all kinds could include respect and dignity.

From Individuals to Organizations

A person can care deeply about children or other needy people and still have a healthy self-interest in avoiding financial exploitation. A person can work "for the money" in business or industry and still bring their values and human social and emotional dimensions to the job.

The present chapter has shown that love and money are not at odds within the context of individual motivations and small-scale interpersonal relations. When we move to a "structural" or "systemic" perspective, though, you might object, there are larger economic forces involved. Many people would claim that even the most sincere and intrinsically motivated individual, or the most well-led and cooperative work group, ultimately must bend to "systemic" forces, such as the dictates of profit maximization. Thus, in the next chapter I turn to the question of behavior at the *organizational* level. When the discussion turns to corporations and markets, must we still see economic life as a machine rather than as a beating heart?

5

BUSINESS *AND* ETHICS?

The Question of Organizational Behavior

The Complexity of Organizations

The last chapter dealt with individuals, their motivations, and their interpersonal relations. Most people have little problem accepting that individuals generally have moral and relational sensibilities. We also realize that people often face real dilemmas and hard choices in choosing and acting on their goals. We know that people often care a great deal about others. The last chapter was about seeing that these aspects of an individual don't just evaporate when a person enters an "economic" situation.

But when it comes to larger organizations, especially large corporations, many people would deny that *organizations* can have any such ethical and caring sensibilities. They also deny that organizations face any dilemmas about their goals. A for-profit organization, they say, *must*—for various reasons I will examine below—have as its exclusive purpose the making of *maximum profit*.

Probusiness advocates tend to glorify the presumed efficiency of for-profit enterprise. They see nonprofit or government organizations as undisciplined and wasteful in comparison. Antimarket advocates tend, on the other hand, to think of for-profit organizations as greedy, while they look more benignly on nonprofits and the state. Nonprofit organizations, they believe, naturally focus on the nonmonetary, usually more service-oriented, goals spelled out in their legal statement of purpose. Government organizations, they believe, look out for the "public good."

For example, I mentioned three hospitals in the last chapter. Many of my antimarket friends would assume that a couple of them are for-profit institutions. The large hospital that bossed my sister around and the Brockton hospital that put the squeeze on nurses seem likely candidates. The fact that "they are interested only in profit" would seem to explain their attitudes toward their staff. On the other hand, my friends would guess that the small hospital that paid attention to the well-being of its staff would be a nonprofit or state institution. When I tell them that this small hospital also ranks higher on measures of patient satisfaction than the large one (though they serve the same population), this reinforces their expectation.

In fact, the for-profit chain in my sister's story is the one with the high staff and patient satisfaction levels. The state institution in her story is the county hospital which almost drove her from nursing. The nonprofit institution among these three examples is actually Brockton Hospital, whose management had exploited its nurses and demeaned them in its public announcements. How can this be?

In reality, we can't make judgments about how an organization will behave simply by looking at what is written on its legal charter. And there is more than just anecdotal evidence that demonstrates this point. While some empirical studies have suggested that the average quality of health care may be lower in for-profit than nonprofit hospitals, for example, others have suggested that there is little difference in quality.[1] A large study of child care centers found no difference on a number of measures of average quality between for-profits and nonprofits in three of the states it looked at. In a fourth state, which had less state regulation, nonprofits on average performed better. In the same study, nonprofit centers run by churches compared poorly with other nonprofit programs—not what you would guess if you think of churches as especially "altruistic."[2]

Averages also can conceal a great deal of variation *within* the for-profit, not-for-profit, and government sectors. (I used to make this point to my statistics classes by telling them about the statistician who drowned trying to cross a stream an average of eight inches deep.) One study of hospitals found that the difference in average mortality rates between for-profit and nonprofit hospitals was swamped by "an enormous amount of variation in mortality within each of these ownership types."[3] That is, even when nonprofits on average perform better, you can still find examples of inferior nonprofits and superior for-profits.

The fact that quality of services and commitment to social responsibility can vary widely among businesses is also well known to activists who monitor them. Advocates who work to raise issues of social responsibility with corporations, for example, report that they encounter a wide variety of responses. Some for-profit businesses are relatively willing to make changes in their operations—or even take the lead within their industry on employee, community, or environmental concerns. Gap Inc., for example, recently won social responsibility awards for issuing an unusually honest report on labor conditions in its clothing factories worldwide, including reports on infractions of its own code. Other companies completely stonewall social responsibility advocates and turn a blind eye to damage they are causing. For example, about the same time as Gap Inc. received its award, another clothing manufacturer—Cintas—took a quite different tack. Cintas responded to a shareholder request to investigate conditions in its factories by suing the shareholder for defamation.

There is too much variety in human organizations to reduce them to simplistic formulas. The purposes their leaders and employees intend to serve, and the degree of success or failure of the organization in carrying out such purposes, vary widely.

So why do organizations behave as they do? To explain this, we need to look at both the outside pressures faced by organizations and at their internal structures. Both probusiness advocates and antimarket critics tend to see for-profit businesses as inexorably *driven* to maximize profits by external forces. I will examine this claim at length and then turn to the issue of how motivations are converted into action *within* organizations.

What Is Profit?

Profit has become a loaded word, so undermined by the mechanical-economy metaphor that it has lost nearly all usefulness in discussions of economics and ethics. At one extreme, cheerleaders for capitalism assume that profits are wonderful because they motivate "wealth creation." The profit motive is imagined to be the almost magical driving force behind ever-greater economic development and growth. At the other extreme, capitalism's critics take profit making to be synonymous with greed and exploitation. They see profit making as leading only to the accumulation of unjust wealth and the oppression of workers. They believe that profit-oriented businesses are morally tainted from the get-go. Any attempt at dialogue between these two sides breaks down because of their divergent beliefs about what profit-driven economies automatically produce.

We can, however, state the essence of profit in more value-neutral terms, which may help us see how dialogue could take place. An activity is profitable if it creates something that is of greater value than the inputs used to make it. In this sense "profitability" is generally a positive thing. A meeting is profitable if the outcome from it is worth the time spent attending it. As a nearsighted person, I'm grateful to people who take inputs of unfinished plastics and metals and create eyeglasses, which are of far more value to me than the original materials would be. I'm writing this book because I hope what I create will be of greater value than the ink and paper and time that are used up in making these pages. An activity that is "unprofitable," in contrast, is a waste, destroying value (or at least creating no additional value).

The vast chasm between the probusiness and antimarket extremes can narrow a bit, if you realize that the central issue is not profit itself, but how you measure *value*.

The market cheerleaders' view is based on the rather untenable assumption that market prices reflect true social value. In order for their story to work, it would have to be true that any good or service that can be sold at a profit increases the real wealth of a society. It is pretty easy to come up with counterexamples, however. Some folks would name items like cigarettes, heavily advertised junk foods, polluting SUVs, violent television shows, or automatic weapons as products that are socially damaging as well as highly profitable. Others might list television shows they consider sexually immoral, Michael Moore's movies, or this book as products for which the market price is higher than the social benefit. Not everything that can be profitably sold is really a good thing.

Another problem with the market cheerleaders' view is that it ignores the fact that market prices reflect only the preferences of those with money to pay. To the extent the provisioning of life is left purely to markets, the rich get their caviar while poor children die for lack of immunizations and clean water. Market prices reflect private, not social, values. Lastly, market cheerleaders blithely assume that there is no social downside to letting the profit chips fall where they may—letting the Bill Gateses of the world accumulate as much personal wealth as the markets give them.

The critics of markets are more insightful in noticing that market value may not be the same as human value and that wealth creation can have negative social effects if wealth is extremely unevenly distributed. But to say that therefore *all* profit making is bad is to kill the goose that lays the golden egg. What I believe ethically conscious people should be arguing instead is that activities should be *socially as well as financially profitable* and that the benefits from wealth-creating activities should be *distributed* in a way that is just and that does not create socially damaging concentrations of power. This is a much more reasonable argument. It leads into questions about the responsibilities of economic actors across the board and away from simply blaming "big, bad business."

If we look at the financial profit motivation as one among *many* influences on economic and social life, then we can find grounds for discussions about how to make profit work for the social good. But, alas, both market advocates and business critics agree that businesses must by their nature pursue a *single* goal: the maximization of profits.

The Notion of the "Alien" Corporation

The idea that business firms are 1 oo percent dedicated to "maximizing profits," at whatever detriment to other possible goals, is commonly stated as fact. I can understand why my mainstream economist colleagues tend to neglect the human and social nature of business firms. Organizations involve real, complicated, human beings and the real social and logistical problems of managing people, information, and operations. This makes them much too concrete and messy a subject for a discipline that prides itself on elegant mathematical analysis. How much easier it is to consider the subject of analysis to be an idealized, unitary, autonomous "firm," whose only action is to find the level of output that makes a mathematical profit function take on its greatest value! Saying what firms "are" and "do" reduces, for neoclassical economists, to sophisticated manipulation of the basic calculation of financial revenues and costs, and the difference between them.[4]

"Firms maximize profits" is not a phrase that came into popular use because economists spent years seriously studying actual business firms. Nor is it based—as will be discussed below—in law. It is a notion that is preferred by economists because it is amenable to the application of calculus. It is a notion that is part of the mythical ideal of a smoothly functioning, perfectly competitive economy. It is popular exactly to the extent that the mechanistic, clockwork image of the economy is taken for granted.

I am a bit more puzzled by why anyone other than my mathematically oriented colleagues would take the notion of single-minded firms so seriously. Simple everyday observation certainly suggests that businesses are far from being smoothly run, profit-maximizing machines. At the very least, many companies are run by (rather human) managers who are far more interested in their own salaries and longevity on the job than in getting the best deal for the shareholders. I would think that the scandals at Enron, WorldCom, and so many other businesses would call into question the idea that corporate leaders always have the general shareholders' interests at heart! Other companies seem to focus more on growth or innovation (think Amazon.com or Wal-Mart) or being on the leading edge of technology than on profits per se. I suspect that for many CEOs the status-seeking goal of getting on the cover of *Fortune* magazine plays a large role. Other businesses explicitly and openly make decisions that trade off the short-term financial interests of shareholders for longer term, less tangible business goals such as improving employee satisfaction or building a positive reputation in their community. Yet other companies are so badly run and chaotic it is hard to detect a purpose in them at all.

But critics of markets also hang on to the "profit maximization" creed. The story from market critics usually goes something like this. Corporations are simply *not allowed* to take the interests of their employees, communities, or the environment into account because, by law, they must maximize profits. Furthermore, even if a corporation *were* for some reason willing to take on some extra costs for the sake of greater social or environmental responsibility, this would be ineffective. Because in competitive markets only the most ruthlessly cost-cutting and profit-oriented firms survive, a firm that tries to be ethically responsible will be run out of business. Thus legal mandates and competitive market pressures force firms to greedily maximize profits, at whatever cost to human and other life. And thus commercial interests can be shown to be intrinsically and directly opposed to human interests.

David Korten, as I mentioned in an earlier chapter, characterizes corporations as "aliens" or "machines." He writes, "Behind its carefully crafted public relations image and the many fine, ethical people it may employ, the body of a corporation is its corporate charter, a legal document, and money is its blood. At its core it is an alien entity with one goal: to reproduce money to nourish itself."[5] He stresses over and over again that corporations are something *other than* organizations of people—that they are something set apart, something driven by forces alien to human aspirations.

An interesting point about this view is that it cannot be challenged with evidence. What if you try to point out an instance of what you see as socially *responsible* corporate behavior? "Merely a public relations stunt," such critics reply. Or "Only temporary— the inexorable forces of market competition will force the firm back in line." A sign of good scientific—including social science— practice is that its theories can be tested against the evidence. A position that is by its nature immune to evidence is not a social science theory, but an assumption, a belief, or a dogma.

At the center of the argument is the belief that profit maximization is forced on corporations by law and by market pressures. Let's examine the facts.

Are Corporations Driven by Legal Mandates?

Corporations have a long and complicated history in law. These days, a corporation comes into being when a group of people properly file a document called a corporate charter (or articles of incorporation) with the appropriate government authority.

In the United States, this is usually a state government. The charter lists details such as the name of the corporation, its purpose, who its directors will be, what kind of stock it will issue, and other provisions. The stockholders (or shareholders) who put up the financial capital for the business are the ultimate owners of the corporation. If the company does well and profits, the stockholders will receive a return on their financial investment in the form of dividends or appreciated stock. The (appointed or elected) board of directors is supposed to guide the (usually hired) top managers of the company.

If firms were legally mandated to "maximize profits" or "get the highest possible returns for their stockholders," wouldn't you expect this to be mentioned in the law in some highly visible place? Yet if you actually look at the relevant state legal codes, what you find is much more vague. The corporate codes usually simply state that a business corporation's purpose is to engage in business or trade. Many U.S. corporations choose to incorporate in Delaware because of advantages in its corporate codes. In the section on formation and purposes in the Delaware corporate codes, the words *profit* or *return* are nowhere mentioned. The articles of incorporation of an individual corporation are often even vaguer, stating simply that the corporation's purpose is "to engage in any lawful act or activity" permissible under the state codes.

You might then turn to case law to see how these laws are interpreted by the courts. Perhaps the *courts* enforce "profit maximization" even if it isn't spelled out in the legal codes?

Case law has established that directors and managers of corporations have a "fiduciary duty" (duty of loyalty or care) to the corporation. This is often interpreted as requiring them to maximize returns to shareholders. Yet, if you look at the actual descriptions of the duties of directors, what you find is a requirement that they must act "in a manner . . . reasonably believed to be in the best interests of the corporation."[6] This, again, is much vaguer—it does not specify that the "corporation" is the shareholders only, nor that serving the "interests of the corporation" means maximizing profit.

Supporters of the profit-maximization view like to cite *Dodge vs. Ford*, a court case decided in Michigan in 1919. Henry Ford, majority shareholder in Ford Motor Company, had decided that, instead of issuing special dividends to shareholders, he would use available funds to expand capacity and employment. This would make cars cheaper so they could be purchased by families lower down the income scale. Minority shareholder Dodge sued. The Michigan court found for the plaintiff, stating that if Ford wanted to pursue altruistic goals, "he should do it with his own money, not the corporation's."[7] "A business corporation is organized and carried on primarily for the profit of the stockholders," the court ruled. "The discretion of directors," the court continued, "does not extend to a change in the end itself, to the reduction of profits, or to the nondistribution of profits among stockholders in order to devote them to other ends."[8] Using the results of this court case as evidence, supporters of the profit-maximization view like to present an image of corporate managers and board members being sued right and left by shareholders should they violate this norm. If corporate officers, say, divert some revenues into improving working conditions or spending on environmental protection—zap! They get served. Or they are fired or thrown off the board. The only safe and legal way to act as a corporate officer, it would appear, is to be socially irresponsible.[9]

While often cited as demonstrating the legal underpinning of "corporate capitalism," *Dodge vs. Ford* is, however, only one snapshot—and an outdated one—from a long-running story of legal controversy and business evolution.[10] In clear contradiction to the usual interpretation of the Ford case, legal scholars note that, in the contemporary United States, "each state implicitly recognizes that a broader group of interests may be considered" and "*no* state corporation code in existence specifies that the directors of a corporation owe a fiduciary duty *solely* to the shareholders."[11] Even in Delaware, significant case law recognizes the rights of corporate directors to consider other interests.[12]

Further, in thirty-two states, "constituency statutes" now exist which explicitly transform the obligations of corporate directors by expanding the groups to which boards of directors are accountable. For example, in Minnesota, the groups in whose interests the directors may act are listed in the statute as "the corporation's employees, customers, suppliers, and creditors, the economy of the state and nation, community and societal considerations, and the long-term as well as short-term interests of the corporation and its shareholders."[13]

Is a corporation legally required to set aside ethical concerns in order to squeeze out the last drop of profit for its shareholders? According to the American Law Institute, "corporate decisions are not infrequently made on the basis of ethical considerations even when doing so would not enhance corporate profit or shareholder gain. Such behavior is not only appropriate, but desirable."[14] A broad reading of contemporary law does *not* simply say that corporations must maximize shareholder value.

Then there is the question of how much effect law actually has on corporate behavior, anyway. People don't just hop to compliance with a law, especially if interpretation of the law is controversial (as in this case) or the law is only loosely enforced. Legal scholar D. Gordon Smith says he is "surprised" by the way his colleagues embrace the idea that corporations are focused on serving their shareholders. The case law on shareholders suing directors for breach of duty, he notes, shows that shareholders face an uphill battle. The directors only need to show that their action can be attributed to "any rational business purpose" to avoid being found lax, even if their decisions in fact led to poor outcomes.[15]

Perhaps even more important, a diverse understanding of obligations is found among corporate directors themselves. One survey found that only a minority of directors felt obligated only to shareholders; most directors feel obligated to more than one constituency.[16] Business scholars Collins and Porras reported in their study of successful companies that "'maximizing shareholder wealth' or 'profit maximization,'" was *not* "the dominant driving force or primary objective" of the "visionary" companies they studied.[17] Providing a *quality good or service, at a reasonable or fair profit*, for example, was a commonly expressed motivation. Yet these companies were all leaders in their fields, in existence for at least fifty years. Their managers hadn't been successfully sued or sacked for neglecting their supposed legal single-minded "duty" of grabbing every last possible dollar for their shareholders.

Lastly, there are important questions about timing and about just what "shareholder interests" are. In the profit-maximization view, shareholders are assumed to be interested only in financial gain, and presumably in fairly immediate financial gain. Yet if you consider, for example, our excessive dependence on depleting stocks of fossil fuels and the associated problem of global climate change, how can the bulk of shareholders *not* have a long-term "interest" in decreasing our economy's reliance on oil and natural gas? Presumably individuals care about future generations of their family, at least. And these days, with many pension funds and insurance companies holding corporate stocks, the ultimate shareholders include you and me.

Making a good faith effort to earn profits is, indeed, one of the important responsibilities of a business manager. But achieving the *highest* profit without regard to *any* other goal is not required by law. If it is not a requirement laid down in law, then where does the idea come from?

It is my tribe, economists, who are the source of this fixation with *maximization*. The phrase "profit maximization," so often bandied about as though it is written into law, actually originated, as far as I can tell from my research, in the methods of mathematical optimization (that is, maximization or minimization) enshrined in the neoclassical economic model. While legislators and judges have, as we have just seen, generally been rather vague about the purpose(s) of business, mainstream economists have been vociferous in popularizing the idea that firms have a single, simple, and (conveniently!) quantifiable goal.

I am not alone in uncovering these economistic roots. Distinguished legal scholar Lynn A. Stout has also traced the popularity of this mistaken idea to economists, and especially to the rise of "Chicago School" economics. (The economist who pronounced that businesses should have no responsibilities beyond making profits, Milton Friedman, is a prominent "Chicago School" leader.) The idea's popularity among legal scholars grew in the late decades of the twentieth century, Stout claims, because the profit-maximization creed expounded by these Ph.D. economists "lent an attractive patina of scientific rigor" to the study of corporations. To the business press, meanwhile, it offered "an easy-to-explain, sound-bite description" of what corporations are and do.[18]

The popular idea that corporations single-mindedly maximize profits does not come from law or the actual observation of business practices. It is an offshoot of economic dogma, plain and simple.

Are Corporations Driven by Market Pressures?

The second objection to the view of corporations as human organizations concerns the pressures exerted on individual firms by the workings of "the market." Even if some individual CEOs might have goals other than maximizing profits in mind, the argument goes, the pressures of competitive markets will sooner or later drive all companies that are not ruthless profit-maximizers out of business.

To the probusiness zealots, this is well and good. The "market discipline" of competition forces businesses to run efficiently, thus increasing wealth.

Antimarket advocates also agree that market pressures drive corporations, though they are less sanguine about the outcome. Companies that try to uphold labor or environmental standards, for example, will incur higher costs and thus need to sell their product for a higher price than their lower-cost rivals. Consumers, who we assume are interested only in getting a good deal, will buy only the lowest-price product. Thus, the responsible firm will go out of business, and only vicious, irresponsible profit-maximizers will remain. Or, instead of looking at competition among firms, we can tell a similar story about competition in the markets where firms get their financial capital. That is, efficient financial markets will cause the managers of any companies that generate less than their maximum potential profit to be sacked and replaced, through hostile takeovers. The global competitive market system runs tight, with no slack.

This is more economic dogma. Competition drives all firms to maximize profits *in the idealized world of neoclassical economics.* That is, in a world in which there are so many buyers and sellers in every market that each has to take the market price as a given, in which firms are interested only in profit and consumers are interested only in their own utility—and in which many other assumptions hold—this result follows. This is the clockwork economy with which so many of my professional colleagues are enthralled. All evidence suggests that real-world economies are much more complicated.

Parts of the global economy are, indeed, highly competitive. The many, many small clothing subcontractors that produce for large, branded companies or major retailers, for example, have to compete fiercely with each other. If they don't say that they can provide the shirts or blue jeans at a bare-to-the-bone cost, the big-company buyer will look elsewhere. For this reason, clothing manufacturing has moved from the United States to countries like Honduras and Bangladesh, and then more recently on to countries like Vietnam and China with even lower labor costs. The situation has been similar for the thousands of companies competing for contracts to assemble electronics and various other goods. When a company is just one of many that can produce a particular item, the company has to take the price offered for its product as a given. Economists say that firms in highly competitive markets have no "market power."

But other parts of the economic system are not so fiercely competitive. Firms have a degree of market power if the goods or services that they produce are somewhat differentiated from what other firms produce. If people believe that Dole canned pineapple is better than a generic brand, for example, then Dole can set its price a few cents higher. Companies also increase their market power if they provide a substantial share of the goods in the market in which they sell, because then the buyers of their goods face limited alternatives. Wal-Mart, for example, is a company well-known for leaning on its thousands of suppliers to cut their costs. But Wal-Mart is hardly a "perfectly competitive," "price-taking" firm itself. It has achieved (at the time of this writing) a substantial 30 percent share of the U.S. general merchandise market. Microsoft's hold on the market for desktop operating system software is even more extreme: its market share is in the neighborhood of 90 percent. Consider General Motors, ExxonMobil, IBM, Pfizer, Verizon, UPS, and the like— these are hardly the anonymous, powerless companies of neoclassical theory. Such companies do not just passively accept the "dictates of the market." They actively strategize about what, where, and how to produce, how to get buyers to prefer their brand of product, and how to set their prices. They may even use lobbying or predatory business practices to try to manipulate the structures of the markets in which they participate.

A subtle point about the neoclassical theory of competition and profits seems to be missed by many who claim that market pressures "force" firms to act this way or that way. To people untrained in neoclassical theory, the idea of "profit maximization" is, quite understandably, associated with the idea of "making really big profits." In the concentrated, big-business sectors of the economy, there are, in fact, many corporations that receive revenues way in excess of strictly necessary costs. Such companies may rack up big profit numbers in their quarterly reports, or accumulate so much extra revenue that they can embark on huge programs of expansion or acquisition, or pay their top directors ridiculous salaries, or make big political contributions to curry favor for their industry. To the noneconomist who argues that market pressures force firms to "profit maximize," these cases may seem to point in their favor. Yet neoclassical economic theory points in the *opposite* direction.

When market pressures are strong, neoclassical theory says, economic profits will be driven to a particular level—*zero*! Under strong competitive pressures, firms will have just enough left over, after paying their workers and their suppliers, to pay a normal, going rate of return to their creditors and shareholders, says neoclassical theory. "Making really big profits" is *not* evidence that a company is being forced to profit maximize by market pressures. On the contrary, it is evidence that the firm has been successful in *protecting itself* from competitive market pressures!

It is the small, weak firms at the margins of corporate capitalism that are most driven to profit maximization by market pressures. Large, multinational corporations operate, on the other hand, largely from positions of market power. They are able to generate revenues in excess of strictly necessary costs and do so over extended periods of time. The economic conditions they face do not dictate their decisions to them: they run with some "slack" and room for discretion.

The question is, what do such companies *do* with the difference between revenues and strictly necessary costs. Technically speaking, the extra revenues are only "profits" if they are reported as such and either divvyed out as dividends to shareholders or turned back into the firm in the form of retained earnings (that, used productively, will increase future revenues, thus causing share prices to rise and giving the shareholders a capital gain). If the law and market pressures really required that companies act only to increase financial returns to shareholders, that is what they would have to do.

But another thing a company running with some slack can do, in actuality, is play around with the cost side. It can raise salaries at the top, increase perks for executives, increase its political contributions to causes favored by its officers, build a sumptuous headquarters building, expand its operations (whether profitably or not), sue anyone who criticizes it, or do other things that aggrandize the wealth and power of its top managers and directors. Sound familiar? The driving force behind such actions is neither legal nor economic: no outside power is forcing decisions to go in this direction. If one has to point to an "energy source" behind such actions, it is clearly just plain old human pride and greed.

Or the company running with some slack could spend more on pollution control, on salaries and wages at the bottom of its pay scale, on assuring that its subcontractors comply with labor and environmental standards, on exploring alternatives to fossil fuels, on company day care centers, on socially useful research and development, or on programs to benefit the communities in which it participates. It could act as a responsible corporate citizen, building up long-term political goodwill on the basis of reputation-enhancing actions. There is no legal or economic "mechanism" that prohibits this.

The directors and managers of corporations that are not strictly under the thumb of fierce competitive pressures—as most of them aren't—*have choices.*

Addressing Objections

The view of businesses as social organizations goes so deeply against the grain of much popular thinking, however, that further objections must be addressed.

The Single-Goal Objection

"OK," someone may reply, "You've made some good points. But asking directors to manage firms with all these different interests in mind is ridiculous! They need a single, clear goal that they can shoot for—like making maximum profits." Canadian business leader William Dimma, for example, claims that the popularity of the view that corporations should pay attention to a variety of interests is based on its "emotional appeal." He believes that its implementation "thrust[s] directors and management into a fuzzy, shapeless world."[19] The answer to this objection, of course, is that life *is* complicated, in business just as elsewhere. The world simply is not an algebra problem, where you always can arrive at a clear, unambiguously correct solution by the bottom of the page. It is sheer illusion to think that life is that simple, anywhere outside of math class.

The Continual Expansion Objection

Or perhaps someone replies, "OK, maybe I said that corporations have to maximize profit. But what I really meant is that corporations are forced to *grow*. Any company that doesn't squeeze its workers so it can continually *expand* will be left in the dust! That's the plain fact!" In this case, the neoclassical-competitive-pressures story (and its counterarguments) becomes irrelevant. But while the neoclassical profit-maximization story has impressive-seeming contemporary intellectual credentials (that is, many Ph.D. economists propound it), the idea that firms are forced to *grow* is of a more uncertain pedigree. The notion of a never-ending drive for growth seems to be rooted back in the Marxian theory of accumulation and has a certain popular cachet. It does apply in the special case of Ponzi (pyramid) schemes, in which early investors are paid out of funds collected from later ones. And it is true that during times of speculative frenzy people sometimes confuse mere expansion with future profitability. But I've not come across in contemporary writings anyone who lays out a detailed and plausible argument for the necessity of continual growth for businesses in general. It usually is argued by mere assertion.

The mergers-and-acquisitions wave of the 1980s might have been taken as empirical evidence for the theory that corporations have to grow, but that period was followed by a period of less of this activity. In fact, some of the earlier highly touted agreements ended in break-ups. It is true that when companies grow they often command more market and political power—and perhaps even benefit from "too big to fail" government policy. Yet very large companies are also generally more difficult to manage effectively, and business analysts have increasingly raised questions about the desirability of mergers. The much-touted merger of AOL and Time Warner, for example, was announced with great fanfare in January 2001. But a year later the difference in products and in corporate cultures at the two original firms had proven to make working together so difficult that stock values had fallen 70 percent. The claim that some unexplained energy or mechanism or "economic dynamic" forces companies to continually grow *ad infinitum* makes for effectively scary rhetoric. But, while there are obviously drives for growth that come out of human thirsts for status and power, the idea that there is an inexorable "economic mechanism"behind corporate growth—à la the clockwork economy—is a matter of belief and speculation, not fact.

Life in Organizations

A corporation, like any other organization, involves real people and the real emotions, ethics, and social relations they bring with them. However, some scholars like to make a significant distinction between "individual-level" and "structural-level" analysis. People may be social and moral, such folks may say, but corporate behavior is driven by the *structure* of business. Such scholars are likely to misconstrue my argument and portray me as missing this distinction and claiming that all we need to do to get nice businesses (or other nice organizations) is to have nice people working there.

If I claimed that, I'd be wrong.

Organizational decision making and behavior is *not* the same thing as individual decision making and behavior. Organizations are complex. For an organization to function, people need to communicate information to each other. Flows of information may be well designed or poorly designed. Managers have to set up incentive systems, drawing on people's extrinsic and intrinsic motivations. Incentive systems may be well designed or poorly designed. Plans need to be made. Meetings need to be scheduled. Decision-makers have to be chosen and decisions have to be made. Then decisions have to be carried out. In addition to formal channels of information and command, informal systems (around the golf course or water cooler) function as well. Between the intentions of nice people and the actual execution of an action by the organization, there are many occasions for slippage! The internal formal institutional structure, informal networks, and culture of an organization create layers of complexity that stand between individual intentions and organizational actions.

How can a corporation become responsible? It must set up internal systems and structures of information flow and ethical oversight consistent with a goal of ethics and social responsibility. Harvard Business School professor Lynn Sharp Paine argues that corporate responsibility is not just a matter of individuals inside having moral standards, but of creating a whole context in which ethical business decisions are facilitated and encouraged. This requires attention to such things as how company performance is measured, how standards are set and enforced, and how work is planned and coordinated. Individual morality must be complemented by a sense that the organization also has moral agency and by the sorts of information flows, incentive structures, and processes that make responsible organizational decisions possible.[20]

For example, consider another episode from my sister's experience in nursing. While she has felt generally well-treated by her current, for-profit employer, she rather resented it when all staff were required to attend a seminar on ethics. She felt she and her coworkers on the floor were already ethical enough! However, at the seminar she learned that the company has a telephone hotline for employees to report any observations of unethical practices. Shortly thereafter, she observed a specialized clinic in the hospital packing in more highly profitable surgeries by scheduling surgeries beyond the normal end of the day. She felt this was dangerous, since many hospital facilities were closing by that time and only on-call staff was in place. She called the hotline. The practice of late-day surgeries stopped. It would have been better, of course, if the hospital decision-makers hadn't tried to pack in so many extra surgeries in the first place. But having a good informational feedback loop in place allowed a person close to the problem to pass on an ethical alert to those people in more-distant decision-making positions. And, apparently, decision-making procedures in this organization have been designed to handle such alerts in a way that can lead to responsible action. A good interior structure within a business can help it achieve both ethical and financial goals.

Or consider the issue of sex and race discrimination. Habermas considered bureaucracies, with their formal layers of power and rules, to be part of the dehumanizing "system." But if you give individual people with all their personality quirks *too much* freedom in making hiring and promotion choices, their unconscious prejudices are given free rein. They'll tend to choose people who are good—but not so good that they make the decision-makers look bad by comparison—and who fit in with them, both socially and in terms of work styles and priorities. In order to make decision making more fair to people who have historically been discriminated against, many now argue that the decision-making process must be structured to be more open and transparent. *Fortune* magazine recently ran an article about how businesses can protect themselves from discrimination lawsuits: "Be much more formal in setting up systems for selection and promotion. Define the required competencies. Always post jobs. Be able to justify your selections."[21]

Some organizations complement this increasing formality with workshops to help decision-makers become more aware of their own unconscious biases and "old boys' club" habits.

Those who oppose individual-level to structural-level analysis usually tend to think about business "structure" in terms of a mechanical image of automatic profit maximization and rigid hierarchy. I believe that taking a more management-oriented approach, and trying to understand how particular *internal relations* affect the complex behavior of organizations themselves, would be more fruitful.

What about Nonprofits?

Some people advocate "protecting" certain activities from "economic values" by having them done by nonprofits or the state. We need to realize, however, that there is nothing *automatic* about these kinds of organizations, either. Human issues and problematic interior structures can lead even nonprofit, public-service-oriented institutions to behave in ways that work against their socially worthy, formally stated purposes.

For example, I once worked at a university that prides itself on "academic excellence." It claims to be a "world-class research institution" that also offers the "intimacy and personal attention of a small liberal arts college." Its Web site brags that it "emphasizes an interdisciplinary approach to knowledge." The university's mission statement says that it "strives to reflect the heterogeneity of the United States and of the world community." All this sounds lovely, doesn't it? This private, nonprofit organization is clearly thoroughly devoted to research excellence and the building of an inclusive and diverse community of learning. Right?

Before moving to this smaller university, I had been tenured (that is, given a lifetime position) at a top-30 U.S. economics department. I had built up a strong research record, as attested to by numerous publications in prestigious journals, and had acquired an international professional reputation that also crossed the academic disciplines. For family reasons, I had left that tenured position and moved to this smaller, less well-known university and department, untenured but with a commitment that I would be reviewed for tenure soon. There was a structure in place for this. My appointment letter said that I would be reviewed for tenure, and the procedures for such a review were spelled out in the faculty handbook. The most generally accepted measure of research in economics, in such formal proceedings, is the quantity and quality of one's published articles, with the rankings of the journals in which those articles appear taken as a measure of quality.

What actually happened came as a shock to me. At first, in spite of what my appointment letter had said, I was denied a promotion review entirely. I was criticized for having small ("intimate"?) enrollments in a new course I had been asked to teach. I was told by the dean that, with regard to the evaluation of faculty performance, "interdisciplinary work doesn't count." Later, the university did a review, but then denied me tenure on the grounds that my research, while it had been sufficient for tenure at a much higher ranked institution, was inadequate by *their* lights. Meanwhile, they tenured a male departmental colleague of mine whose top publication was in a journal ranked 104th in the profession. The year I was let go, the economics department hired five new full-time faculty. Although the initial denial of a review had been based on the argument that my "fields didn't fit their needs," one of the new people hired was in the fields I had taught in at my previous university. All the new hires were male. In spite of this institution's worthy stated goals, I believe that it was bias against women and an aversion to my challenging of the macho biases of mainstream economics that was behind their actions. [22]

Yet I would not single out this university as being particularly unusual. Rather, it has been my experience—in *every* organization I've been a part of—that organizations are extremely complex. It may be a nice fiction to think that everyone in an organization is 100 percent devoted to carrying out its stated mission and that all procedures are well designed and flow smoothly. But if you are inside an organization and reasonably aware of the emotional and social dynamics around you, you find a complicated human mixture of greed, fear, warmth, respect, passion, support, coldness, courage, devotion, confusion, jealousy, confidence, prejudice, backstabbing, brownnosing, high ideals, loyalty, competence, sincerity, camaraderie, accomplishment, disagreement, opportunism, incompetence, generosity, creativity, inconsistency, mediocrity, moral bankruptcy, ethical leadership, cross-cutting purposes, petty turf squabbles, unexpected synergies, and personality conflicts. You find internal practices that lead to useful meetings, accurate communication, good assignments of responsibility, fair rewards, and efficient actions and others that lead to useless meetings, miscommunication, dropped balls, unjust rewards, and inefficiency. Sometimes the presumed overt purpose of the organization is accomplished pretty well, sometimes it is accomplished in part, and sometimes it is completely undermined.

Isn't this true? Have you ever spent time in a workplace, school, religious or civic organization, or family—any organization, whether "for profit" or "not for profit"—that didn't demonstrate at least *some* of this human and structural variety?

Organizations and Goals

I fully agree with the market critics' point that goals other than making money should be important. But I fully disagree with the sort of "separate spheres" idea which says that we can judge an organization simply by what is written on its legal charter. The fact that an organization is run as a "for profit" in no way requires, either by law or by economic "mechanisms," that it must have profit as its *sole* goal. Nor does being run as a nonprofit or "in the public interest" guarantee good motives or outcomes. Organizations must be evaluated by *what they do*.

When you think about it, it is no surprise that the evidence about organizations and outcomes should be so mixed. It is not just for-profit businesses that, since they have to keep an eye on their costs, may be at times tempted or forced to cut corners on employee benefits, the quality of what they create, or their responsibilities as community citizens. Nonprofits and government-run programs have to meet a budget too—and often (especially in human services) a stingy one. And it is not just for-profit organizations that might be run by insensitive, greedy, or short-sighted people or suffer from bad institutional design.

My point is not, of course, that for-profit businesses can simply be trusted to act in an ethical way. My point is that *all* sorts of organizations require an active attention to ethics and oversight from concerned outside groups. Once we drop the idea of the economy as an automaton, we realize that *nothing* is simply automatic.

6

KEEPING BODY
AND SOUL TOGETHER

So Why Does This Matter?

Probusiness, neoliberal zealots firmly believe that the economy is a machine. They assert that any direct concern with ethics or care is unnecessary because a market economy *automatically* serves the common good. Antimarket critics also believe the economy is a machine. They assert that ethics and care are impossible within capitalism since the system *automatically* runs on the energy of self-interest and greed. Either way, the metaphor forces us to divorce the "body" concerns of economic provisioning for our lives from the "soul" concerns of social responsibility and caring relationships. The economy-as-machine metaphor has blinded us to the real-world qualities that make humans work and care and organizations run. Yet the metaphor is quite unnecessary. We *can* join together our legitimate values about provisioning and job creation with our legitimate values concerning ethics and care. The metaphor of the economy as a beating heart may be helpful. A beating heart circulates the lifeblood that sustains physical bodies, while the heart is also traditionally considered to be the seat of the soul. The heart is the symbolic seat of courage, as well, which we will need if we stand up and take responsibility for our economic actions.

But so far the discussion has been mostly about how people think and the words they use. What difference does how we think about economics make for our *actual lives*, personally and as a society?

Bringing—and keeping—body and soul together is critically important for two hugely important areas of our lives. An aversion to thinking about money when the topic of discussion is care has led to a crisis of resources in the caring sectors of the economy. An aversion to thinking about ethics when the topic is business has, on the other hand, led to a crisis of responsibility in commercial life.

A Crisis in Care

It is not overstating the case to say the United States is facing a crisis in care. Consider the various ways in which children receive care. Paid child care suffers from serious problems of quality and availability. A recent nationwide study of cost and quality in randomly selected child care centers rated only 24 percent of preschool centers (usually serving children ages 3 to 5) as good to excellent. Most centers were rated as minimal to mediocre. Some 40 percent of infant care centers were rated worse than mediocre, giving care of such inadequate quality that children's safety was potentially jeopardized.[1] One of the big problems leading to low quality is high staff turnover, averaging about 40 percent per year nationwide. And one of the problems leading to high turnover is low pay. According to a 1998 government survey, only 17 occupations (out of 774 surveyed) have lower average wages than child care work.[2] Or what if a parent wants to stay home for a bit after the birth of a child? Unlike the vast majority of industrialized countries (including Canada) the United States has *no* national program to financially support parental leave, even for a few days or weeks. Most cities have long lists of children waiting for a place in a foster home.

What about the frail elderly? A 2002 study prepared for the Department of Health and Human Services reported that staffing levels are inadequate in 90 percent of the nation's nursing homes, putting residents at risk for problems such as bedsores, dehydration, and malnutrition. Wages for nursing home aides are very low, and turnover rates among nursing home aides are high—amounting to almost 100 percent within the first three months.

And how well do we care for the ill? To read the media reports, the United States suffers from a nearly chronic shortage of hospital nurses. Hospitals claim that they can't get enough qualified people and have increasingly come to rely on minimal (or subminimal) staffing, mandatory overtime, and nurses recruited from abroad to keep their operations running. Nurses (and many doctors as well) complain that they no longer have the time to actually observe, talk to, and understand their patients, or to help make them comfortable and allay their anxieties about medical procedures. Understaffing has been linked to increases in errors, resulting in increased illness and even death.

I believe that a good deal of this problem is due to a carryover of the Victorian expectation that hands-on caring work should be "free" and flow copiously from natural springs of altruism. We just aren't used to the idea that caring involves *skilled work* as well as an other-regarding emotional bent. We aren't used to the idea that people who do carework might have financial responsibilities for their own families. We even suspect that asking for a living wage is a sign that a worker is greedy and uncaring. What a load of bunk! The time and money that go into caring have *always* required economic support, even if in Victorian days that support was covert and indirect. It is time that we made economic support for caring work direct and *sufficient* to support it at a quality level that doesn't give us nightmares.

We should, I believe, as citizens, support legislation that seeks to upgrade health and child care quality by setting standards for staffing levels, staff qualifications, and pay. We should support unions and other organizations of caring workers in their fights for decent working conditions and fair rewards. Managers of hospitals, nursing homes, and child care centers should take an active role in studying "best practices" and designing industry standards that work. We should take another look at how we care for the elderly and consider more seriously how good home care and hospice care might often create a better quality-of-life than our current, more medically oriented system. We should value more highly the caring skills demanded in other fields as well, such as primary education and social work. The United States should follow the example of nearly every other industrialized country in helping a parent afford to stay home or find quality paid care during an infant's early life.

Some will object, of course, that raising financial support for caring work is not "affordable." This comes from a shortsighted, bake-sale mentality. Finding money to fund improvements in hands-on care need not be a matter of trying to pull fresh money out of a hat. As any economist will tell you, economic decision making means making choices. As a society, we seem to find money for billions of dollars in government- and insurance-supported pharmaceutical purchases and payments for expensive medical tests. Why is it, then, that *spending time* with patients is "unaffordable"? Regarding child care, one estimate puts the cost for a subsidy plan (including quality incentives that would allow for better pay) in the United States at approximately $26 billion per year (over current spending).[3] This will seem outrageously expensive if your point of comparison is "free" child care provided invisibly, by unpaid and underpaid women. Yet numbers in the high millions and into the billions are commonly bandied about at the local and federal levels when the topic of discussion is transportation (U.S. federal spending on transportation currently totals $57 billion), the Department of Defense ($402 billion), or other projects. Many other countries subsidize child care to a far greater extent than does the United States. Only when we realize that it is the nurturing and sustaining of *life* that we are talking about, not frills, will we start taking the economic support of care seriously.

Rather than arguing that care shouldn't be done "for money," we should be arguing *for* money: for money to support those individuals and organizations in charge of protecting, nurturing, and healing the most vulnerable among us.

A Crisis in Business

Enron Corporation looked bad enough. The energy corporation had lobbied hard that regulation of utilities should be replaced by "free markets" during the 1990s and then rode the crest, reporting high profits. High-ranking executives got millions of dollars in bonuses. But in the fall of 2001 the apparent health of the company was revealed to be due to massive accounting fraud. Debts had been hidden in sham partnerships. The scandal spread to the accounting firm of Arthur Andersen. The company collapsed. Small shareholders—including Enron employees who had invested heavily in Enron stock for retirement—found their holdings worthless.

But Enron was not the end. A year later Forbes.com's "Corporate Scandal Sheet" listed not only Enron and Arthur Andersen but also Adelphia Communications, AOL Time Warner, Bristol-Myers Squibb, CMS Energy, Duke Energy, Dynegy, El Paso, Global Crossing, Halliburton, Homestore.com, Kmart, Merck, Mirant, Nicor Energy LLC, Peregrine Systems, Qwest Communications International, Reliant Energy, Tyco, WorldCom, and Xerox. And the Forbes list was limited to purely accounting scandals over only about a year. It doesn't include the insider-trading scandal at ImClone or other fraudulent activities uncovered at AES, Cendant, Citibank, JPMorgan Chase, Merrill Lynch, PricewaterhouseCoopers, Rite Aid, and Vivendi Universal. Years later, the list still seems to grow all the time. The business, accounting, and regulatory communities have been thrown into a tizzy of discussions about accounting standards, securities regulation, executive pay and stock options, corporate governance, and business ethics. You don't need to read more than the front page to see that corporate financial fraud is a hot issue.

While a handful of ideologues still try to twist these scandals into evidence that "free markets" work, those not so fond of tortured logic readily acknowledge that commerce is in need of concrete reforms toward greater accountability, transparency, and ethical standards. Few people would claim, in the light of these crises, that a smooth invisible hand makes the naked greed of business officers work for the social good. And these discussions are largely about the ethics of business leaders vis-à-vis the general shareholders—the very group whose interests, in the mechanical view, were supposed to be *automatically* and seamlessly served by the corporation!

Then there are the issues of corporate responsibility toward workers, customers, communities, and the environment. The local business news lately in my community has been about how Bank of America promised not to cut jobs when it bought out a local New England bank. Shortly thereafter, it eliminated 2,900 jobs in the area. (It is now slowly adding some jobs back as it faces public pressure.) Kraft Foods has just announced, after years of pressure from health advocates, that it will stop advertising junk food to young children. Today's headlines held news about controversies over environmental standards for perchlorate, a toxic chemical byproduct of the manufacture of rocket propellant. In the world news, reports of human rights abuses, environmental destruction, and corruption linked to corporate activity (sadly) abound. Labor unions, community activists, environmentalists, "fair trade" groups, health advocates, consumer advocates, charitable and social service groups, "watchdog" agencies, and religious groups are working hard to raise public awareness about social and environmental issues.

I believe, however, that the "machine" rhetoric that often accompanies revelations of corporate irresponsibility actually retards achievement of good goals. Think about it. *Corporations are huge, grinding machines. Their actions are inexorable. They are invading aliens . . . cancers . . . blights.* Where is the power in such imagery? It is with "them," the Goliaths. Meanwhile, it leaves "us"—the damaged parties, activists, or simply concerned human beings— in the role of helpless victims. "We" are left with an image of needing to struggle to get the economic machine into "our" power—or destroy it—before it destroys "us." Meanwhile, mechanically minded activists expect nothing but animosity and opposition from those in places of power in corporations. They expect nothing better from them—in fact, their whole theory says that business leaders *cannot* act ethically due to the machine or alien nature of the corporation. While such rhetoric makes for high drama, I believe that being a bit more pragmatic and open— and less self-righteous—would get activists a lot further.

When *outside* pressure has been effective in changing the behavior of a corporation toward greater social responsibility, it is generally because such pressure has supported the agendas of people *inside* the corporation who share the same goals. Respecting the ethical capabilities of people inside the corporation means that advocacy groups can see their role as one of both conflict *and* cooperation—of both challenging current practices *and* working with those business leaders who can actually effect change. This makes advocacy much more powerful. In the purely adversarial view, tiny groups of outside advocates must try to *force* change upon a big, powerful, evil, and unwilling corporation. If instead we see corporations as human organizations, the role of an outside advocate is to be the goad, the watchdog, or the burr under the saddle of *people* within the corporation, people who can keep the organization from getting too complacent.

In this more realistic view, we can recognize both the substantial contribution made by outside activists and the fact that real change can come only from within. Bill Shireman and Tachi Kiuchi, for example, are leaders of an organization that fosters business/activist dialogue. They have found that, when both sides shed their "black-and-white preconceptions about one another" and "set aside [their] fear of talking to 'the enemy,'" win-win solutions can often be uncovered.[4] Corporations that take the lead in social and environmental responsibility could—and should—also raise these issues within their industry associations and wherever else their voices are heard.

Instead of assuming that outside "structures" of law and competition "drive" corporations to maximize profits, a view that considers both internal and external structures as evolving processes would be more helpful. As individuals, we often feel overwhelmed by the large scale of economic, political, and social systems. But, looking at the broad historical sweep, we can also recognize that these systems evolve. Monarchies went out of fashion as democracies evolved. Today's corporate capitalism is very different from the entrepreneurial capitalism of Adam Smith's day. It is true that the structures of social and economic life shape us as individuals, but it is also true that as individuals and as people working together we, over time, in turn shape the structures.

Regarding external pressures on corporations, critics of corporations call for many reforms that I can endorse. It might be a good thing for corporate boards to be encouraged to be more responsive to the various stakeholders by incorporating worker, community, and other representatives. It might be helpful if, as some activists propose, states would rewrite their laws so that corporate charters more explicitly require social and environmental responsibility. I don't think that diversifying boards or rewriting charters is a cure-all, but these actions could be helpful. We can as individuals support changes toward greater social and environmental responsibility by participating in consumer boycotts, shareholder actions, and buying "fair trade" products. As citizens, we can lobby for better laws and regulations that bring pressure to bear on corporations, in the direction of a more just and sustainable society. As citizens, we can also support a return to a more progressive, pre-Reagan, system of taxation that could help prevent extreme concentrations of economic power.

In addition to creating external pressures on corporations, developing good structures of information flow and accountability *inside* corporations is critical. Internal structures can work either with or against the people inside corporations who want to act responsibly. "Triple bottom line" or "social impact management" accounting systems that include social and environmental as well as financial criteria are promising lines of development. It would be naive to think that financial and social/environmental concerns *always* point in the same direction. There will always be plenty of room for consumer and government action to bring financial incentives more closely in line with social values. But recognition that business decisions *are* ethical decisions starts us on the right path.

A Way Forward

I don't expect mainstream scholars in the social sciences and philosophy to lead the way toward a more adequate understanding of the relations among economics, ethics, and care. Academe just has too much inertia. While I'd love to have it otherwise, I strongly suspect that ten years from now many beginning economics students will still be taught that the economy is a wonderful machine.[5] I suspect that many beginning sociology or philosophy students will still be instilled with a fear of the presumably inherently dehumanizing effects of monetized exchange.[6]

Instead, I believe that it will be people on the ground, working in business management or doing the work of care, who will be most helpful in breaking down the petrified eighteenth-century image of the economic machine. I hope that, over time, more scholars and popular writers will support the project, shifting public opinion toward a new and more responsible view.

A lesson from history may be useful here, too. In the late 1800s, at the start of the Progressive Era in U.S. politics, the battle lines seemed clearly drawn. On the one hand, the "robber barons" of capitalism—the owners of big steel, big oil, and the like—built huge fortunes in the unregulated, free-wheeling capitalist markets of the time. Meanwhile, the industrial workers—some of them children—worked fourteen to sixteen hours a day in unhealthy, oppressive conditions. It would seem that the workers would be poised to respond to the Marxist call, "workers of the world, unite!" Yet the guiding philosophy of the Progressive Era was that the interests of capital and labor did not *have* to be seen as strictly opposed. We owe many things we take for granted today, such as labor laws, regulations on financial markets, programs such as Social Security and unemployment insurance, and food and drug inspections to innovations made during that era. The programs themselves were generally designed using input from *all* the interested parties. Commissions including representatives from industry, labor, consumer groups, and government agencies were set up to work out solutions to the worst problems afflicting the industrial economy of the time.

Institutional economists, of whom the most famous was John R. Commons of the University of Wisconsin, played a role in spreading this pragmatic approach in the early decades of the twentieth century. Commons and his colleagues were not guided by any grand theory that gave them answers in advance of actual investigations. Their methods relied heavily on looking at the specific nature of particular industries and problems, gathering information on what sorts of solutions had been tried elsewhere, and seeking the input of concerned parties. Not surprisingly, such a pragmatic approach was looked at suspiciously by mechanically minded purists on both sides. On one side, radical Marxists objected that it merely made an inherently oppressive system a little more bearable by throwing more crumbs to the workers. On the other side, champions of capitalist wealth creation grumbled that the government "interference" created by Progressive policies put an unnecessary drag on free-market forces.

Now, in the early twenty-first century, it is time to retrench. Some of the old Progressive policies, designed for the industries and families of their era, don't fit our situation so well anymore. We need new social responses to deal with new issues. Ecological issues weren't on the radar screen yet, back then. Care was assigned, unpaid, to women in the home when the Progressives designed their policies. But right-wing purists are now threatening to roll back many of the Progressive Era programs entirely and put nothing in their place. They spout ideologically inspired neoliberal, promarket policies that prescribe deregulation and privatization in all spheres. Marxism has meanwhile all but lost its teeth as a critique of this, as disappointing results in communist countries have made radical theory a mostly academic exercise. While the policies created by the old Progressives are no longer entirely adequate for today's society and economy, I think we can learn a great deal from their methods. "What are the greatest causes of harm in today's society?" and "How can we work together to correct them?" are the right questions to ask.

The response to one kind of mechanical purism need not be the opposite variety of mechanical purism. We can recognize that the health of living, vital economies depends on our ethical decision making and our willingness to support relationships of care and respect. If we want a world of social justice, ecological sustainability, and care for those who need it, I hope we will, like the Progressives of old, put our efforts toward the pragmatic and challenging project of making real-world economies work for human benefit. Our bodies and souls depend on it.

Notes

Introduction

1   William J. Baumol, *The Free-Market Innovation Machine: Analyzing the Growth Miracle of Capitalism* (Princeton, NJ: Princeton University Press, 2004), chap. 1.

2   David C. Korten, *The Post-Corporate World: Life after Capitalism* (San Francisco: Berrett-Koehler; West Hartford, CT: Kumarian, 1999), 23, 36.

3   Adrian Walker, "Foster Parents Deserve a Raise," *Boston Globe*, March 20, 2000.

4   For those readers to whom these things are important, the graduate school was the University of Wisconsin, Madison; the government agency was the U.S. Bureau of Labor Statistics; the department in which I was tenured was the University of California, Davis; and I have published in journals including *Econometrica*, *American Economic Review*, *Journal of Political Economy*, *Journal of*

Economic Perspectives, Review of Economics and Statistics, and *Journal of Labor Economics.*

Chapter 1

1   Adam Smith, *An Inquiry into the Nature and Causes of the Wealth of Nations* (1776); excerpt in *The Essential Adam Smith,* ed. Robert L. Heilbroner (New York: W. W. Norton, 1987), 159.

2   Adam Smith, *The Theory of Moral Sentiments,* ed. D. D. Raphael and A. L. Macfie (1759; Oxford: Clarendon, 1976), 182, 185, 186.

3   Smith, *Wealth of Nations,* book 1, chap. 2.

4   Smith, *Wealth of Nations,* book 4, chap. 2.

5   Smith, *Theory of Moral Sentiments,* 185.

6   John Stuart Mill, *Essays on Some Unsettled Questions of Political Economy,* 2nd ed. (London: Longmans, Green, Reader & Dyer, 1874), essay 5, pars. 46, 38.

7   I will examine some of the assumptions behind this theorem in the next section of this chapter.

8   I skip over opposing schools of economic thought, including Marxism, Institutionalism, socioeconomics, and Austrian thought, since, in spite of their insights, these schools have relatively little following within contemporary academic or popular discussions of economics. Also, many mainstream economists will think that my portrayal of the discipline is too stark, pointing out that neoclassical economists have stretched the core model in many directions since the time of its invention. This does not take away from my point. One need only look at the "core" curriculum at both the undergraduate and graduate levels to see that the neoclassical model in its simplest form is still considered *the base* on which the rest of economics is built. Also, even when the neoclassical para-

digm is stretched in new ways, the new additions tend to be mere modifications or "tweaks" of the basic mechanical metaphor. In the last few years, for example, there has been a rising interest within economics in the neurophysiology of emotions. Potentially, such a dialogue between economics and psychology could bring renewed attention to people's physical bodies, personal and social values, and complex, evolved behaviors. Instead, however, the psychological information has been absorbed into the model of rational choice, with the emphasis being put on how emotions might cause people to make "mistakes" in their processes of (otherwise) rational utility maximization. In my more academic writings, I have engaged with many and varied aspects of contemporary economics, but my point here is to examine only the core metaphor.

9   For a promarket, somewhat mechanistic, discussion by an economist that yet takes into account some of the complexities of real-world market institutions, see John McMillan, *Reinventing the Bazaar: A Natural History of Markets* (New York: W. W. Norton, 2002).

Chapter 2

1   Center for Career Development in Early Care and Education, "Briefing Booklet: Advance Reading for Sept. 14, 2000," Wheelock College, Boston, MA.

2   John Atherton, "Where Do Spirituality and Economics Meet?" *Journal of the Association of Christian Economists* 17 (1994): 10, 11.

3   David Korten, *When Corporations Rule the World*, 2nd ed. (San Francisco: Berrett-Koehler, 2001), 23, 74, 223; Nancy Fraser, "Rethinking Recognition," *New Left Review* 3 (2000): 11; David Loy, *The Great Awakening: A Buddhist Social Theory* (Boston: Wisdom, 2003), 42, 67, 80; Ken Jones, *The New Social Face of Buddhism: A*

Call to Action (Boston: Wisdom, 2003), 161–62; Barbara Kingsolver, *Small Wonders* (New York: HarperCollins, 2002), 13; Virginia Held, "Care and the Extension of Markets," *Hypatia* 17, no. 2 (2002): 32; Gar Alperovitz, "Sustainability and the System Problem," *The Good Society* 5, no. 3 (1995): 3.

4   Korten, *When Corporations Rule the World*, 245; Herman Daly and John Cobb Jr., *For the Common Good: Redirecting the Economy toward Community, the Environment, and a Sustainable Future* (Boston: Beacon, 1989).

5   Marjorie Kelly, *The Divine Right of Capital: Dethroning the Corporate Aristocracy* (San Francisco: Berrett-Koehler, 2001).

6   A leading academic proponent of this view is Michael Walzer, *Spheres of Justice: A Defense of Pluralism and Equality* (New York: Basic Books, 1983).

7   Max Weber, *The Protestant Ethic and the Spirit of Capitalism*, trans. Talcott Parsons (London: Allen & Unwin, 1930), 181.

8   Jürgen Habermas, *The Theory of Communicative Action*, vol. 2, *Lifeworld and System: A Critique of Functionalist Reason*, trans. Thomas McCarthy (Boston: Beacon, 1981).

9   Habermas, *Theory of Communicative Action*, 113, 173, 202, 402.

10 Arlie Russell Hochschild, *The Commercialization of Intimate Life: Notes from Home and Work* (Berkeley: University of California Press, 2003), 8.

Chapter 3

1   Thomas Kuhn, *The Structure of Scientific Revolutions* (Chicago: University of Chicago Press, 1962).

2   George Lakoff and Mark Johnson, *Metaphors We Live By* (Chicago: University of Chicago Press, 1980), 5.

3   Evelyn Fox Keller, *Reflections on Gender and Science* (New Haven, CT: Yale University Press, 1985); Susan Bordo, *The Flight to Objectivity: Essays on Cartesianism and Culture* (Albany: State University of New York Press, 1987); Sandra Harding, *The Science Question in Feminism* (Ithaca, NY: Cornell University Press, 1986); Brian Easlea, *Witch Hunting, Magic and the New Philosophy* (Brighton, UK: Harvester Press, 1980).

4   Keller, *Reflections*, 53; James Hillman, *The Myth of Analysis* (New York: Harper & Row, 1972).

5   Many of my economist colleagues will strongly protest this characterization. Indeed, some economists do useful, applied work on issues such as poverty, wages, taxation, business cycles, and actual real-world markets. I would argue, however, that in most cases the usefulness of their work comes about largely *in spite of*, instead of *because of*, any use they make of the mechanical paradigm. At high levels of academe, however, economists are fairly well protected from any need to prove themselves useful. The faculty in leading departments generally review each other's work and hire each other's graduate students. Thus, they can set their standards about what is valuable—and fashionable—largely in-house.

6   Many of us who are academics and writers feel sincere concern for the needy of the world and feel that our writing is the best way we can contribute to a better world. A business leader who is offended by our criticism may well reply to us, "So how many people did *you* grow food for today? How many jobs have *you* created for the unemployed?" Point taken. In material terms, the work of a writer mostly uses up trees.

7   Economist Nancy Folbre has also suggested bringing a "heart" metaphor into discussions of economics: *The Invisible Heart: Eco-*

nomics and Family Values (New York: New Press, 2001). While I have benefited enormously from her work, I should point out important differences in our use of this image. Folbre suggests that the "invisible heart" of "love, obligation, and reciprocity" undergirds the functioning of the "invisible hand" of "decentralized, automatic, self-regulating forces . . . in competitive markets" (xii). That is, she takes the "invisible hand" as given and argues for the importance of an *additional* image. In contrast, I use "a beating heart" as a *single* metaphor that includes the provisioning function and the regularities of economic life as well as care (and courage). I consider the "invisible hand," with its implied automaticity and exaggeration of competitive forces, to be an often-misleading abstraction rather than a description of a true, behind-the-scenes, independent reality. I therefore do not include it at all in my suggested imagery.

8   For academics studying economies, this diversity means giving up on the idea of a "grand theory" and reaching, instead, for more modest and useful "midlevel" theories. Part of the appeal of the mechanical model to academics has been its (illusory) comprehensiveness, based in the idea that economies could be described by simple, eternal, geometry-like truths. Giving up the idea that economics is like geometry, however, does not at all require that we give up the quest to better understand economic life. Continuing with the heart metaphor, we could think of the empirical and experimental practices of biology and medicine as examples of fruitful models for economic research.

9   As with any metaphor, the characteristics of "a beating heart" do not literally match up one-for-one with characteristics of an economy. The "economy as clockwork" metaphor was never meant to suggest, for example, that an economy has hands or tells time. Likewise, among the associations I do *not* mean to suggest are that economies are thoughtless (drawing on the old "head" versus

"heart" imagery) or that they can be replaced by machines (artificial hearts). No metaphor is ever complete.

10 Milton Friedman, *Capitalism and Freedom* (Chicago: University of Chicago Press, 1982), 133.

11 Korten, *When Corporations Rule the World*, 74.

Chapter 4

1 Both quotes are from Teresa Toguchi Swartz, "Mothering for the State: Foster Parenting and the Challenges of Government-Contracted Carework," *Gender and Society* 18, no. 5 (October 2004): 583.

2 Happily, in this particular case, the rules were changed a year later to allow for continued health coverage and a small stipend, and the Hernandez family adopted the boys (Swartz, "Mothering for the State," 583).

3 A recent survey of health care managers confirms the prevalence of this view. See Julie A. Whitaker, "The 'Heart Issue': Health Care Managers and the Discourse of Compensating Wage Differentials" (working paper, University of Wisconsin, Madison, 2004).

4 Habermas, *Theory of Communicative Action*, 270, 266, 272.

5 See Mervyn King, "The Institutions of Monetary Policy," *American Economic Review* 94, no. 2 (2004): 1–13.

6 Richard M. Titmuss, *The Gift Relationship: From Human Blood to Social Policy* (London: Allen & Unwin, 1970).

7 Bruno Frey, *Not Just for the Money: An Economic Theory of Personal Motivation* (Cheltenham, UK: Edward Elgar, 1997).

8 Howard Margolis, *Selfishness, Altruism and Rationality* (Cambridge: Cambridge University Press, 1982).

9   Kathy Modigliani, *Child Care as an Occupation in a Culture of Indifference* (Ph.D. dissertation, Wheelock College, 1993), 22.

10   Folbre, *Invisible Heart*, 38.

11   "Brockton Nurses Plan to Walk Out as Contract Talks Fail," *Boston Globe*, May 25, 2001. The nurses stayed on strike until September 2001 and called off the strike only after the hospital agreed to a number of concessions concerning staffing, mandatory overtime, inappropriate floating, and pay.

12   Julia O'Connell Davidson, "The Rights and Wrongs of Prostitution," *Hypatia* 17, no. 2 (2002): 86.

13   James C. Collins and Jerry I. Porras, *Built to Last: Successful Habits of Visionary Companies* (New York: HarperBusiness, 1994), 228; emphasis in original.

Chapter 5

1   For an example of a study that finds differences on average, see P. J. Devereaux et al., "A Systematic Review and Meta-analysis of Studies Comparing Mortality Rates of Private For-Profit and Private Not-for-Profit Hospitals," *Canadian Medical Association Journal* 166, no. 11 (May 28, 2002). For an example of a finding of little difference in quality, see Frank A. Sloan, Gabriel A. Picone, Donald H. Taylor Jr., and Shin-Yi Chou, "Hospital Ownership and Cost and Quality of Care: Is There a Dime's Worth of Difference?" *Journal of Health Economics* 20, no. 1 (January 2001): 1–21.

2   Suzanne W. Helburn, ed., *Cost, Quality and Child Outcomes in Child Care Centers: Technical Report* (Denver: University of Colorado, Center for Research in Economic and Social Policy, 1995).

3   Mark McClellan and Douglas Staiger, "Comparing Hospital Quality at For-Profit and Not-for-Profit Hospitals" (NBER Working

Paper 7324, National Bureau of Economic Research, August 1999).

4 In recent decades, some relatively mainstream economists have begun to try to take into the account the organizational nature of firms. "New institutionalist" economics and transaction costs economics, however, still share many neoclassical assumptions. Profit maximization is still seen as the sole goal of the firm (though now certain difficulties in achieving it are recognized), and the models still work with a very limited set of imagined human relations. Meanwhile, the neoclassical assumption of the perfectly unitary firm continues to dominate teaching and be the default assumption for the bulk of economic research.

5 Korten, *When Corporations Rule the World*, 74.

6 D. Gordon Smith, "The Shareholder Primacy Norm," *Journal of Corporation Law*, Winter 1998, 285.

7 Quoted in William A. Dimma, "Putting Shareholders First," *Ivey Business Quarterly* 62, no. 1 (1997): 33.

8 Quoted in Smith, "Shareholder Primacy Norm," 278.

9 See, for example, Kelly, *Divine Right of Capital*, 148.

10 Discussions of responsibilities of corporations to parties other than their shareholders were lively in the 1930s. See Lynn A. Stout, "Bad and Not-So-Bad Arguments for Shareholder Primacy," *Southern California Law Review* 75, no. 5 (2002): 1189–1209. The discussion resurged in the 1980s, following a formulation of the problem by the influential business administration scholar R. Edward Freeman, in *Strategic Management: A Stakeholder Approach* (Boston: Pittman, 1984). These debates have centered around the question of whether a corporation's purpose is to provide profits for its *shareholders*, or whether its actions should also take into account the interests of others who have a stake in the firm, who

have been called the firm's *stakeholders*. Employees are one obvious group of stakeholders, but suppliers, customers, creditors, and local communities also commonly have a considerable stake in the corporation, having made long-run plans and firm-specific investments based on the corporation's continuing in business. At the time of this writing, the debate is resurging once more, sometimes phrased in terms of the "property model" versus the "entity model" of the firm (Stout, 1190). The notion may be further expanded as well: Society as a whole may also be considered a stakeholder, to the extent that the firm's actions have more widespread social or economic consequences. Firms also have a reciprocal relationship with the natural world: they are not independent of the influence of natural disasters, ecological degradation, or ecological improvement, and their actions in turn affect the ecological balance.

11 Edward S. Adams and John H. Matheson, "A Statutory Model for Corporate Constituency Concerns," *Emory Law Journal* 49 (2000): 1088; emphasis added.

12 Jill Fisch, "Measuring Efficiency in Corporate Law: The Role of Shareholder Primacy," University of California—Berkeley Law and Economics Workshop, 2004, paper 5 (available at http:// repositories.cdlib.org/berkeley_law_econ/Spring2005/5/; accessed July 25, 2005).

13 Adams and Matheson, "Statutory Model," 1085, 1087.

14 American Law Institute, *Principles of Corporate Governance: Analysis and Recommendations*, 1994; excerpted in "Managerial Duties and Business Law," Harvard Business School Publication No. 9-395-244, July 1995.

15 Smith, "Shareholder Primacy Norm," 286.

16 Jay W. Lorsch and Elizabeth Maciver, *Pawns or Potentates: The Reality of America's Corporate Boards* (1989), as cited in Smith, "Shareholder Primacy Norm," 291.

17 Collins and Porras, *Built to Last*, 8.

18 Lynn A. Stout, "New Thinking on 'Shareholder Primacy'" (working paper, University of California at Los Angeles School of Law, January 10, 2005), 4–5.

19 Dimma, "Putting Shareholders First," 33.

20 Lynn Sharpe Paine, *Value Shift: Why Companies Must Merge Social and Financial Imperatives to Achieve Superior Performance* (New York: McGraw-Hill, 2003).

21 Betsy Morris, "How Corporations Are Betraying Women," *Fortune*, January 10, 2005.

22 My dispute with this university was eventually resolved using lawyers, mediators, and the Massachusetts Commission Against Discrimination (who ruled that my complaint had "probable cause").

Chapter 6

1 National Association for the Education of Young Children, "Cost, Quality and Child Outcomes in Child Care Centers: Key Findings and Recommendations," *Young Children* 50 (1995): 40–44.

2 Center for the Child Care Workforce, *Current Data on Child Care Salaries and Benefits in the United States* (Washington, DC: Center for the Child Care Workforce, 2000).

3 Suzanne W. Helburn and Barbara R. Bergmann, *America's Childcare Problem: The Way Out* (New York: Palgrave, 2002), 213.

4 Bill Shireman and Tachi Kiuchi, "On (Not) Firing into the Crowd: Five Myths that Fuel Anti-Corporate Hate Campaigns," *Business Ethics*, Fall 2004, 4–5.

5 This is not for lack of personal *trying* to make a difference in the teaching of economics. See Neva Goodwin, Julie A. Nelson, Frank Ackerman, and Thomas Weisskopf, *Microeconomics in Context* (Boston: Houghton Mifflin, 2005).

6 While this is not the place to get into a long review of the academic literature, there are some parts of academe (outside of economics) where challenges to the mechanical notion of corporations have been gaining ground. Interested readers are advised to look into the fields of business ethics and organizational behavior, usually taught in business schools; economic sociology and the sociology of organizations (particularly in its "New Institutionalist" form—which is not the same as "New Institutionalism" in economics), usually taught in sociology departments; and business law, usually taught in law schools.

Index